THE DIGITAL MYSTIQUE

How the Culture of Connectivity Can Empower Your Life—Online and Off

@SARAHGRANGER

Foreword by Elisa Camahort Page,
Cofounder of #BlogHer

SEAL PRESS

The Digital Mystique
Copyright © 2014 Sarah Granger

SEAL PRESS
A Member of the Perseus Books Group
1700 Fourth Street
Berkeley, California 94710

Library of Congress Cataloging-in-Publication Data is available.

ISBN: 978-1-58005-514-7

10 9 8 7 6 5 4 3 2 1

Cover and interior design by Domini Dragoone
Printed in the United States of America
Distributed by Publishers Group West

For my mom,
who showed me that it's possible to be an author,
entrepreneur, and parent, while making it all look easy

And in memory of my dad,
without whom I wouldn't have taken the first leap
toward technology, the Internet, this book,
and my own digital future

CONTENTS

FOREWORD

 By Elisa Camahort Page,
Cofounder of BlogHer

In 2006 Betty Friedan died, and my mother told me that Friedan's book, *The Feminine Mystique*, had changed her life. Inspired and empowered by that book, my mom entered the workforce and forged an entirely new path for herself, becoming my role model in the process. My mom was at the forefront of a cultural revolution . . . second-wave feminism.

In 2006 another cultural revolution was picking up steam: the digital revolution. New levels of access and new tools were driving an entirely new way of connecting and communicating online. A new way to be heard. And it was particularly inspiring and empowering for women and minority segments of the population who felt otherwise unheard. Locked out by traditional gatekeepers.

All of this new opportunity can be both exhilarating and intimidating.

I may be the cofounder of a digitally-native company, but I can relate.

I am not a digital native. Born in the final official year of the baby boom, I didn't touch my first computer until I was out of college. I didn't have an e-mail address until I was thirty-three, nor did I put the "personal" in "personal computer" until I was thirty-eight.

Ironically, I worked in tech, helping deliver to market the equipment that delivered the Internet to homes. But until 2003 it was more theory than practice for me.

Ten years ago, that all changed, and I hopped on the social media train early. In fact, before it was called social media!

I was that person patiently explaining that no, being a blogger didn't mean I sat in a basement in my pajamas telling you what I had for lunch.

And yes, I really had made good, true friends online, despite never having met them in real life.

I've tried to explain things like blogs, Twitter, Instagram, Pinterest, and Google Plus to a wide range of those I call "regular people." It's not easy to show.

How I believe something as simple as a Yahoo! Group for owners of cats with kidney disease helped me extend my cat's life to twenty years old.

How women from all walks of life are making money for their words and their work. Money that buys their groceries or pays their rent . . . or just enables them to go out to dinner every now and then, or feel less stressed about money day-to-day . . . even during the toughest economic times in most of our adult memories.

How people dealing with the hardships we usually keep to ourselves . . . post-partum mental health issues, infertility, grief, loss, illness, parenting challenges . . . are finding a circle of 24/7 support that doesn't exist in what geeks affectionately call "meatspace" (aka IRL, in real life). A community of people who *opt in* to talk about the tough subjects and can always be found. Day in. Day out. In the wee hours. When you know you can't bend your best friend's ear or cry on your partner's shoulder one more time.

How online tools have facilitated revolutions. And social change. And given everyone a voice. You don't have to *listen* to every voice. Not everyone will listen to yours. But everyone with a mobile phone, library card, or other access to the Internet can get online and change the(ir) world.

Online has become my go-to space for every aspect of my life, truly integrated. And it has brought me knowledge, entertainment, friendship, support, relationships (including my significant other), and ultimately my life's work in BlogHer.

Call me utopian, but I think everyone can find that kind of fulfillment and value navigating the Internet, and Sarah Granger can help you chart your course.

Sarah has been online even longer than I have and is at the forefront of many of the new uses for the World Wide Web. I have seen Sarah leverage the power of digital networks and communications for the personal, the political, and the professional. And I have invited her to many BlogHer conferences to share her knowledge and her advice on how we all can traverse this space as gracefully and effectively.

You may be wary of the downsides and pitfalls. You may be scared of the time suck or invasion of your privacy, perhaps the degradation of your offline community.

But you are in control of your destiny here! Use this book and Sarah's guidance to be the one in charge of—not in thrall to—the wonders of an online life. Use this book to find the inspiration and empowerment enabled by this new cultural revolution.

You'll be glad you did.

CONNECTING IS JUST THE BEGINNING

"Mystique is rare now, isn't it? There aren't that many enigmas in this modern world."
—Benedict Cumberbatch, English actor

The summer of 2005 found me in a distressing place. I was on vacation in London with my husband—and was six months pregnant with my daughter—when I started experiencing Braxton-Hicks contractions. It wasn't the first hiccup of the pregnancy. I'd had a mild hemorrhage during the first trimester. Fortunately, after an uncomfortable flight, we made it home to California.

The contractions continued the following week, more than four an hour, so I went to the hospital to be examined. Driving there, every possible worst-case scenario ran through my head. What if I gave birth early? What if my baby couldn't breathe on her own? The doctors confirmed the early contractions, but I was sent home with medication, destined for bed rest. I had cut back on clients as a digital media strategist due to the early hemorrhage that had led to an earlier bed rest during the first trimester, so I found myself in an unusual position of having nothing to do except lie on the couch and worry. Luckily, I had grown up with computers, so my first reaction was to go online.

With my laptop resting on my swelling belly, I clicked away, seeking answers to my questions and comfort for my concerns. What is the difference between Braxton-Hicks contractions and the "real" ones? How do new mothers cope with raising preemies? I found myself on the March of Dimes website, exploring their "Share Your Story" community, a place where pregnant women and new parents blogged about their experiences with early contractions and/or preterm labor as well as premature births.

As I read these blogs by other women like me, I felt an immediate connection. It was as if I were suddenly reunited with long-lost friends. I felt at home, no longer alone on my couch. And although I spent a lot of time feeling fearful of the unknown, crying over the stories some women shared of babies they had lost and some who overcame incredible odds, it still felt better to be in the virtual company of others who understood my concerns. As the weeks passed, I celebrated completing each week with these women, and I edged closer to a safe delivery date. When they were sad, I commented on their blogs with encouraging words. When I shared my fears, they lifted me up. I became a part of this very real, very necessary community online.

Once I reached thirty-seven weeks, I relaxed a bit, knowing that my daughter was in the safe zone and that my pregnancy was now considered full-term. I looked forward to giving birth so I could get up off the couch and figure out a new normal as a parent. Little did I know what I was yet to face. My daughter was born two weeks late, and I suffered complications during delivery that injured some major pelvic nerves, causing excruciating pain. So instead of jumping off the computer and into motherhood, I sank into a serious depression. I was unable to sit without feeling like I was on a bed of nails or stand without feeling like there was an anvil in my abdomen. This left me dejected, scared, and even more alone than before, while attempting to care for my newborn daughter.

The blog that I had assumed I would easily abandon became a new source of comfort. Because those women knew and understood pain and loss, I didn't have to hide what I was going through like I did when I spoke with people in my offline life. (Let's face it—most people just wanted to see photos of my new baby and hear about how happy I was to be a new mother.) Somehow, it was easier to be myself, knowing there was no professional connection that might suffer or personal friend I might alienate.

During the first year of my daughter's life, I was in so much pain I couldn't even stand up long enough to wait four minutes for the toaster to toast a piece of bread. It was too painful to walk from the kitchen to the living room couch, so I often opted to lie on the floor. I'll never forget how humbling it was to lie there, eyes closed, imagining I was somewhere other than my kitchen floor.

So again, in order to have an outlet away from my physical pain, I turned to blogging. A new blog had just launched where I live called The Silicon Valley Moms Blog. I thought, *Hey, I'm a mom in Silicon Valley. I've blogged before. Why not give it a try?* I started slowly, gradually writing about parenting, Silicon Valley culture, daily life, whatever seemed to fit the blog. Then as I became more comfortable, I began writing on other topics like the arts, technology, politics, whatever interested me.

I found my voice as a blogger. The blog was my outlet, allowing me to focus my mind away from the pain. I started my own blog at Sairy.com, based on a nickname a friend had given me in high school. Eventually, I started another pseudonymous blog about pudendal neuralgia, the diagnosis I received for my nerve injuries and pelvic pain. I didn't post there often, but I shared what I could about what I was going through with all of the various treatments I tried that failed and how I persevered onto the next.

I slowly began healing from what would become a long-term chronic pain condition—but the progress was incredibly slow. For each day of a normal person's recovery from pregnancy, it took me a year to cover the same territory. As my daughter grew into a toddler, I began blogging for more sites and resuming my work advising organizations on how the Internet and social media could help them. I gained momentum blogging for a few of these organizations and for *The Huffington Post*, and I became involved in the BlogHer blogging network. I made friends, and I found a renewed purpose.

This wasn't my first experience with the digital world. Far from it. My dad bought our first computer, an Apple II+, when I was nine years old. "This is the future, and I want you to learn it," he said as I stared wide-eyed at the shiny new machine on the table. I quickly became enthralled by the mystique of the computer and its potential. My natural curiosity, blended with the continuing evolution of technology, challenged me to master an understanding of the hardware and software, learning programming skills and network architecture so I could visualize what was happening behind the magic curtain of the monitor screen. As I learned more, I was enraptured by the power of the technology and what it could do for my life and the lives of others. Enabled early by these tools, I became a first-generation digital native.

By age ten, I was chatting with neighbor friends by modem. At fourteen, I made friends from all around Kansas City through local bulletin board systems (BBSes) including my first boyfriend. At seventeen, I secured my first Internet e-mail address. By nineteen, I was studying computer engineering while working as a part-time system administrator in college. By age twenty, my first major paper about technology was published, followed by several online articles.

After graduating, I followed my tech dreams to Silicon Valley, where I worked in IT and Internet startups, followed by several years as an online communications and digital strategy consultant. By the time I gave birth to my daughter at age thirty-two, Facebook was gaining traction in the social media world. I joined Twitter the following year. That's the abridged version of my digital life. The real story is told through the relationships I built through these technologies along the way.

Community is what makes the Web what it is: connections between tens, hundreds, thousands, millions, and billions of people. While the Internet often connects us one-on-one, it also introduces us to new networks and provides endless opportunities for exploration, learning, and sharing. If we don't want to share, we don't have to share. The best part is: we get to choose.

After I became an active member of the Kansas City BBS community in 1987, I met a girl named Angi, who quickly became my best friend. She got married a few years later and we lost touch. I went off to college in Michigan, where I spent most of my time on my umich.edu Internet account, out of reach from the KC BBS world. Years passed and our lives changed, but I often thought of her. One day, twenty years later, she found me on Facebook. I can't begin to express how happy I was at the moment I received the alert. It was like discovering a long-lost sister. I accepted her invitation immediately, we were instantly reunited as if no time had passed, and now we keep in touch often. That one renewed connection with one person made it worth all of the hours I had spent traversing the digital universe, and that is only one example of how my life has been enriched through these connections.

Thirty years after I first ventured online as a nine-year-old, I came to realize that I was no longer just one node on a small network. As a blogger, I became part of something truly amazing—an enduring community of people from all walks of life who supported each other through a wide range of challenges. There is no way to quantify that kind of nurturing community. My daughter is now eight years old, and many of the women who befriended me during those trying first two years after her birth are still my close friends. My online support network became the source of my offline sanity, and that's what brought me through the pain and its companion, depression. More than that, my outlook changed. I'd always been an advocate of the power of the Internet in supporting causes, campaigns, and initiatives, but I hadn't taken the time to stop and think about how it could help individuals in their daily lives. The digital universe—the Internet and everything connected to it through wires and airwaves—is full of these communities. Millions of them. Combined with the brilliance of the technology itself, these communities comprise the source of the real mystique, opportunity, and possibility.

I did not choose the title of this book, *The Digital Mystique*, without carefully considering the obvious comparison to *The Feminine Mystique*. Whereas Betty Friedan's exploration of the feminine mystique centers on a mysterious, unreachable feminine concept, the digital world we'll examine is ripe with a different kind of mystique—elusive and exciting. The beauty of this comparison is that women dominate social networks, and collaboration—generally considered a feminine trait—is at the core of this emerging digital construct. I believe we have an unprecedented opportunity to open up and democratize communications and communities online through collaboration, aiding in a grander cultural movement toward equality for all through a forum where anyone can participate. *The Feminine Mystique* is about breaking cultural barriers; *The Digital Mystique* is about opening new cultural doors.

What was once only possible to say to someone by a letter carried for many months by ships across the sea can now be transmitted through the air in a matter of nanoseconds. We now have the ability to expand our horizons, deepen our relationships, and learn more about our world than ever before. This is the true power of the Internet—connecting people at a personal level. It's about helping others, improving each of our lives, gradually, online, with a variety of tools developed over many years. Now is the time for you to engage online and create new meaning for your life in the process. By reading and acting on the stories, examples, and lessons in this book, your life can become richer and fuller online and off, in ways you may not be able to imagine right now.

I never planned to become an expert on online life, a social media influencer, or a digital thought leader. The mere concepts didn't exist when I first learned to program computers. I just wanted to do something that mattered, and learn along the way. None of this would have happened without that first computer and the nudge my dad gave me to try it out and explore. From there, the digital mystique took over, and the path of my life changed completely. Now it's your turn, and I look forward to our journey together.

CHAPTER ONE

.YOU

"I am so clever that sometimes I don't understand
a single word of what I am saying."
—Oscar Wilde, Irish writer and poet

I'll call her Glenda—my friend since age five.
We grew up in the same neighborhood, attended nearby schools,
shared many ups and downs through our awkward teen years, and
stayed in touch as adults. She got married, spent most of her twenties raising her three kids, then went back to college to finish her
degree after her youngest child was in grade school. When she first
joined Facebook, her goal was to build an online presence for her
business as a family therapist. She felt scared, and she came to me
with questions about how much to show about herself, what to write,
what not to write. I was just glad to see her online. I encouraged
her to experiment, but I understood her concerns and did not think
it made sense to push her too far. She started out slowly, keeping
her personal account totally private, only using it to connect on her
business page with potential patients.

Three years ago, she got divorced, and she found herself with
more time and a new sense of freedom. After a couple of months,
she started sharing more photos on Facebook with family and close
friends. She began texting me jokes and e-mailing me ideas. I could
see her slowly coming out of her shell and gaining comfort online.

When she remarried two years later, she realized she needed to update her digital persona for her new last name and blended family. She found the nuance behind creating digital content to be frustrating at times, but she was savvy enough by then to understand the importance of getting it right. Her new online identity reflects who she is now, and it's helping her stay in touch with family and friends, as well as build her business.

Every time you go online, websites indirectly ask the question, "Who are you?" Each site gathers information about you in order to determine how best to address your needs, and each visitor viewing information you post wants to know a little more about what makes you tick. Developing your online persona is an important first step in your journey, regardless of how actively you manage your digital identity.

Rather than entering into a philosophical discussion about the essence of you, take a look around your house, apartment, or any personal space that defines you. Think about the personal choices you have made so that this space reflects you and your personality. That's what you want your digital home to reflect. That's what this chapter is about—building a digital identity that is true to how you see yourself. That helps others to find and learn more about you.

Over the past ten years, I've spent a lot of time advising various types of leaders on social media strategy for their professional lives. Many of these leaders have public lives as elected officials or advocates. I don't ask them what they want their Twitter account to say or how often they want to post on their blog. I ask them what their vision is and what their goals are. We all have goals in our personal and professional lives, and we all have ideas of the images we wish to show our friends and colleagues.

Through this work, I've learned that often it takes time to teach people why showing themselves online is worthwhile. I've encountered a great deal of fear—some of it warranted, some of it not—and the common theme is to worry too much about what other people think and expect and to shut down thoughts of self-expression online because of the impression that criticism is much harsher in this environment. I'd like to dispel this notion and take several steps back before we get to the subject of engaging with other people. First and foremost: It's your life, and you can control your image online. That includes any content created by you or written about you, photos of you, audio files of your voice, and videos.

Introducing .YOU

The minute you step into the digital domain—whether you call it the Internet, the Web, or some other name—you begin leaving footprints. I don't mean this to sound eerie; it's more like stepping off a plane onto a new continent. It's exciting to visit, and you can't wait to see places, meet people, explore new sights and sounds. Because of the architecture of this new continent, your footprints are tracked, measured, logged, and analyzed instantly by computers. Most websites, applications, and networks automatically keep records of what you do there in order to be the most useful to you and in order to build better future applications and to personalize your experience on their sites.

Robert Scoble and Shel Israel, authors of *The Age of Context*, refer to the "five forces . . . mobile, social media, data, sensors, and location." These can be viewed as five senses through which you can be identified. Physical devices that you use matter too—your computer, smartphone, or any other devices you use that connect to the Internet (your car radio, health monitoring bracelet, whatever)—are all included in the equation, as part of what's known as the Internet of Things. Each thing connected to the Internet, whether it's a Kindle or a kid, produces activity online that's categorized and computed, producing a bigger picture of who's doing what in the digital world.

Once you reach your online destination—for example, a travel blog—you can read and comment on the content on that site. Your comment becomes a lasting record of your digital journey, a part of what the Web knows as .YOU. You have a choice: Do you want the Internet's records, data collected by applications and used by search engines, to create a picture of you that is comprised only of fragments

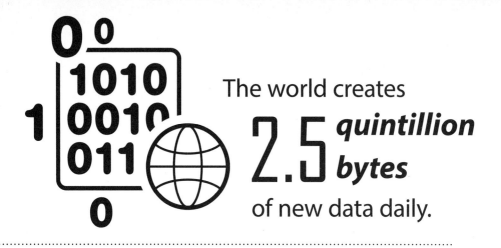

The world creates **2.5** *quintillion bytes* of new data daily.

of content that you leave here and there, like footprints and candy wrappers? Or do you want to build a digital identity that suits your persona, created, curated and controlled primarily by you?

At any point in your digital life, you can actively choose to create new content, planting a flag on this new continent. You can move the flag around until you decide where to build a home, or you can use social networks to build one for you. If you're like most people, you already have an e-mail address and at least one social media account, like Facebook. You've surfed the Web, you've liked some posts, you've shared some articles. That's what the digital world can show others about you. Some people don't see the need to go beyond that point, and that's fine, but I suspect you want to do more, and it's likely you have already.

Building a digital identity takes time. I started out so early online that I didn't consciously ponder the concept for several years, until websites became mainstream. By then, I had my own website, domain, and several e-mail addresses. A few years later, blogs came along, followed by social networks. Ever the digital connoisseur, I tried them all. Now if you search for me online, you'll find thousands of entries, in addition to plenty of content about other Sarah Grangers (such as a 19th century LDS/Mormon women's rights leader, a novelist in the gay romance genre, and a parenting columnist). But since I've taken the time to craft the right kinds of digital content, the first entry that comes up for me is my website—the first room I want people to see when they visit my digital home. Anyone who wants to learn about me can go there; it's the seat of my digital identity.

Owning Your Digital Identity

There are a few important things you should consider doing if you want to carve out a space for yourself online. Centering around your name usually makes this process easier. When I was trying to decide on domain names and business names a long time ago, a good friend of mine, Laz Potter, who runs a web design and development business, gave me a great piece of advice. He said: "Your name is how people remember all that you do. It is always attached to you, no matter where you work. Put your energies there." So I did.

I was lucky enough to be online at an early point in the life of the Internet because I was able to purchase three domains that relate to my name: sarahgranger.com, grangers.com, and sairy.com. If I had been quicker about it, I could have probably bought sarah.com when I was in high school, but the idea didn't occur to me. One of my high school friends was quicker—he bought dan.com, scoring major geek cred, and you can bet he'll keep that domain for the rest of his life. So if you can get a domain with some version of your name or nickname followed by .com or even .net or .org, go for it. Even if you just reserve it and point it to another website or Facebook page later, it will make finding you much easier for people. And it's fun to have!

This approach also translates to naming conventions with social networks. I have facebook.com/sarahgranger and Twitter.com/sarahgranger and Linkedin.com/in/sarahgranger. I still have a five-letter domain, sairy.com, and the username @sairy on Twitter, but for professional use, I knew that I wanted search engines to find my articles and projects via my name. Now everything is at sarahgranger.com or @sarahgranger or some sort of /sarahgranger on social networks, if they were available when I signed up. I wish I had them all matching, but I link them all on the home page of my website, so anyone who wants to find me on those social networks can easily do so. Be as consistent as you can so your friends can find you more easily.

Creating your online presence is like building a house—your front door and entry area should be whatever primary digital destination you choose, like your website, Tumblr page, About.me page or Facebook page. Each social network you join is akin to adding a room to your house, connected to that main entry. Your Instagram room could be a photo gallery including your favorite family memories; your Twitter room could be a collection of interesting books and articles you share with your followers. All of these different "rooms" in your house will fit together as a colorful mosaic of your online life.

Think about Oprah. She's often used as an example of a successful woman for a variety of reasons. Everyone knows who she is and what she stands for, and she has worked hard to make that happen. So if you search for "Oprah" online, you'll find that the first search results that come up are all owned and controlled by her—they are all rooms in her online house. You'll see oprah.com, The Oprah Show, and the Oprah Winfrey Network, OWN. On the day I searched for her, the next entry was her Twitter page—more content controlled by her. After that was her Wikipedia page and her Internet Movie Database (IMDB) page, both edited by others.

Now, you may think that this is meaningless because you don't have the resources that Oprah has to create a website, but that's not completely true. Search engines are configured to look for content you create, websites can be built for free, most social networks are free to join, and they look for original content linked to names, so it is possible to become the first name listed when someone searches for you online.

Most of us have become so accustomed to searching the Internet, we don't think about how search engines actually work, but they are pretty incredible tools. One of my college friends figured out early (around 1994) that Internet search would become increasingly more important, so he went on to study the topic in graduate school. I remember him describing the challenge of search to me: It took immense amounts of space and computing power to store enough information to search the entire Internet, so he wanted to figure out how to do it more efficiently. The result of his research: Google. His

Search Engine Optimization (SEO)

Search engines seem to contain a great deal of digital mystique, but the truth is that search engines are just computer programs. They work based on highly defined algorithms orchestrated to find the best content for each search. As a result, the practice of Search Engine Optimization (SEO) evolved to hone your digital content so that it accurately attracts search engines. SEO has changed over time and will continue to change as search engines are refined and search technology advances. The following is advice from Jaelithe Judy, an SEO expert and blogger whom I've worked with in the past:

> To boost search traffic, you should focus on making your content current, relevant, and authoritative.
>
> **Current** means frequently updated. Search engines do not want to provide outdated information to their users.
>
> **Relevant** means your content should be highly relevant to the specific topics you expect your potential readers or customers to search for. If you were searching for the subject matter that you wanted people to see, what would you type into a search engine? Make sure that those words appear somewhere, clearly, in your writing, preferably in an important and visible place, like the title or the URL of a blog post.
>
> **Authoritative** means you should position yourself as a voice of authority on your subject of choice. Search engines want to send their users to good, reliable sources of information. So ask yourself two questions: 1. How long has the provider of this information been around? 2. How many other people already consider this provider to be an authority?
>
> It's also helpful to link to your own content from other sites or social media accounts you control. For example, if as a blogger you write a guest post on another blog, include a link back to your own blog.

name was Larry Page, and along with Sergey Brin, he revolutionized how we search the Web.

Have you ever "googled" (searched for) yourself online? What did you find? It's useful to do this every so often so you know what other people can see about you. This is often called a "vanity search," but I think of it more as a reflective search, a necessary process to maintain your awareness of what your online footprint has become.

Entering the Realm of Social Networks

Of course web search isn't everything, but it's a good place to start the conversation. You don't need to have an actual website—say, jane-elizabethdoe.com—with photos of you and information, but you do need to think about where you want your primary home to be. Where's the first place people will look for information about you? Do you want them to find you first on Facebook? LinkedIn? Do you want a blog? Of U.S. adults who are online, more than 67 percent are now on social networks. Some 71 percent of women online use social networks, and 62 percent of men use them. Social networks now come in a variety of forms, but each has a different style and type of audience.

Facebook users tend to be used more by women, generally over age twenty-five, emphasizing personal relationships; Google Plus users are primarily men sharing information and images (although this is changing); MySpace tends to be more for artists and musicians; Twitter lends itself to a wide range of people but focuses mostly on news and media and the sharing of real-time events; LinkedIn targets specifically professional connections and leans more male; Path is ostensibly for "close friends" and has a variety of sharing mechanisms including sharing whatever music you're listening to at the moment; Foursquare shares location-based information—where you ate for lunch, or what gallery you visited while traveling. These social networks started out with basic information sharing or answering the simple question: "What are you doing?"

Choosing the right online home for you stems from what your goals are, and you have to keep in mind that the roles of these types of sites change over time. But I don't want you to get hung up on that right now. For most people, I'd suggest either a website, a blog, or a Facebook page. If it helps for you to keep visuals in your mind while pondering these concepts, pick one of those as your image for your online home.

Putting the Personal in Your User Profile

Now think about what you want to have in your online home that reflects the parts of you as an individual. What images do you see? Put together photos of you, your family, you with friends, your physical home, your pets, your work, your hobbies, your activities, and your favorite things. Gather those images into one place. You don't necessarily ever need to post them online, but it will help you put together a picture of what best represents you. And if you already have a website or a Facebook profile, take a look at what you have there. What's missing that might show a more well-rounded picture of you to your friends and colleagues?

The next step is to draft a basic written profile. You may not need this for every social network, but it helps you clarify what you're showing to the rest of the world. According to a University of Texas study, "self-reported personality traits are accurately reflected in online social networks such as Facebook." In other words, the pervasive culture online is to be authentic about who you are offline when you're online. Remember that when working on any profile summary or blurb online.

If you prefer short and sweet, you can aim for 140 to 160 characters, like something that would be on Twitter. If you prefer longer, you can write a 2 to 4 paragraph bio about yourself. The point here is to put together some of the primary pieces of information you would like to share. You can make it just the facts, or you can have fun with it. Remember: It should reflect your personality and your goals for being online. I usually start by making a list of terms or phrases I want to include. Here is an example of what I could use if I were selecting keywords for a draft profile:

SARAH GRANGER

Author, speaker, social media pioneer, blogger, entrepreneur, techie, connector

Wife, mother, figure skater, arts lover

World traveler, lives in Silicon Valley, originally from Kansas City

Now you can see how this easily translates into a social media profile. I typically tweak these terms and create a profile that is current, relevant, and authoritative, stemming from SEO best practices. I choose what I include based on the number of characters or words allowed in the profile summary and what the average length of profiles tends to be. For Facebook and Google Plus, it's longer. For LinkedIn, it's more of a professional summary, and, for Instagram and Twitter, it's more succinct.

Here's another example that I like to share. Katie Stanton is a friend of mine who I admire for many reasons, not the least of which is her ability to create short and (literally) sweet profile summaries. Here's her Twitter bio:

Twitter Globetrotter. Mom of 3. Macaron connoisseur.

Katie (@katies) is the International VP at Twitter, and she's currently living in Paris. She travels the world on behalf of the company and focuses on expanding Twitter's reach. She's brilliant, she's an actively engaged parent, and she's a lot of fun. So rather than just creating a bland profile that says her title is Vice President, that she worked at the White House, and that she's got kids, etc., she had some fun with her profile, picking a favorite dessert that reflects where she's living. When she was in California, her profile read "cupcake connoisseur." Now it's macarons (not to be confused with macaroons). She uses three short descriptive phrases to illustrate the various aspects of her life. And although there's much more to her than what she selected to showcase, you can learn that by reading her tweets.

Another friend of mine, Cynthia Liu, has a more detailed but still creative and informative profile summary. She's a parent, an education advocate, a blogger, and a filmmaker. Her profile reflects each of these things, without being overbearing.

Eat. Mother. Write. Read. Re-write. Film. Repeat.
Project Involve Fellow, 2010. Writer/dir, ALIEN ABDUCTION
(about our fear of the Other).

Writing a good profile summary about you can take time, so don't expect it to be perfect the first time you write it, and don't expect it to stay the same forever. Change is part of life, so our online profiles will evolve to reflect those changes. The keys to writing a good summary or bio are: 1) be authentic, 2) be clear and concise, 3) allow a little flavor. That flavor can be a nickname, a hobby, the place where you live, an organization you work with, a favorite food, or whatever else you think will help others remember you—but it should be something unique. And always remember that you know your story best. You can tell that story online in whatever form you feel most befits who you are and what you want to achieve with your time online.

Profile summaries generally come in handy for social networks like Twitter, LinkedIn, Facebook, Pinterest, and Instagram, as well as personal websites and blogs, where you'll generally want to have a longer bio. Another place you can create a mini-profile is in your e-mail signature, if you so choose. Most people just use signatures for professional communications, but sometimes people will put a favorite quote along with their name, e-mail address, and phone number at the bottom of e-mail messages to add flavor and to clearly display basic contact information.

Strike a Pose—Profile Photos

Here are a few quick tips about selecting profile photos. First: Only post photos that you would be comfortable having published in the local or national newspaper. If you are featured in a newspaper, that's where they'll go to find images of you. And really, don't you want to show only your best face to people who know you anyway?

Second: Please do me (and everyone else) a favor, and don't use a photo of you that has half of someone else's head cropped out of it. Take a little more time and find a good photo that doesn't have you physically attached to another person. If you don't have one, find someone to take one. You'll feel better about it later. (In some cases, I think it's fine to have a photo of you and your husband, for example, as your Facebook profile photo, but I generally advise against including another person in your photo unless that person is directly associated with you by most anyone who knows you.)

Third: If you have children, think very carefully about whether you want photos of them posted publicly with you. This is an area where some parents have differing opinions and make various choices, but remember that once those photos are public, they can be archived online, and, even if you remove them, people may be able to find them. We will go into this more in Chapter Four: The Kids Are Online, but realize that these are important personal choices that you make when you are creating your online persona.

Some other tips about photos of yourself online: Think about how much skin you're showing. This we'll cover a bit in the chapter about engaging with professional colleagues online, but just remember that these days, prospective employers (and customers) will look you up online. If they see a photo of too much cleavage or belly, or, if you're a man and you happen to have a photo without a shirt, just remember that, even if it was no big deal at the time and the photo was at a friend's pool or on vacation or whatever, these photos can be seen by anyone. Make sure profile photos are tasteful, and, when you do share more casual photos with friends, think twice before publishing the ones with too much skin. There are private areas online where you can get away with that, but, as a general rule, just don't do it.

The Key Ingredient—Authenticity

Authenticity is the key to a successful digital life. In my twelve years of blogging, this is the most important lesson I have learned. The more you are willing to show who you are as a person, the more fulfilling your online experiences will become. But this doesn't mean you have to start out by blurting everything about yourself to the world online. Pick and choose the parts you want others to see. This is one of the best things about our lives online—we do have control over a great deal of what is shown about us. Take a moment and think about what words your closest friends would use to describe you. Those are some of the aspects of the authentic you.

Studies are now finding that people tend to show their true selves on Facebook. I think this is a good thing. Sometimes this takes a little bit of courage, but I'll show more examples throughout the book as to why this is helpful. I like to think about it in terms of reciprocity. If you show others more of yourself, they will in turn do the same for you. Then relationships deepen and everyone gets more out of their interactions and time invested online. Remember, you control your life online. What you put out there about yourself is inevitably your choice.

The Sharing Culture

The people who first built the Internet worked in government and universities and did it in the spirit of information sharing. That's why it's easy to connect new devices to the Internet. We all want to find information, learn, and explore, and most of us also want to share. Sharing is a part of life, whether it's sharing where you went to dinner with a friend, your favorite recipe, or your opinion on an important issue. All of these things require putting a part of yourself out there and being actively engaged, even if just a little bit. Sharing is a term that's used a lot when describing what people do online, but it should not be discounted. It is one of the most important concepts behind the world online, just as it is offline.

Like kindergarteners standing up and sharing during show-and-tell for the first time, adults learning to share in the digital world can find it scary at first, and it's okay to be cautious, taking it slowly. The communities you find on the Internet—on websites, blogs, and social networks—are just like offline communities in that you might want to take some time to observe and get to know them first before sharing too much. When you do begin sharing your own thoughts, images, and ideas online, keep in mind the concept of getting out of it what you put into it. I learned this concept as a volunteer in various organizations and later as a blogger. For me, social media has been the gift that keeps on giving, in a real way, because the sharing economy reaps many benefits for all who participate. Just remember to start slowly and build up your content gradually over time.

I'm naturally an introvert, and I sometimes have difficulties talking to new people in person. When I first started frequenting BBSes online (much like today's blogs), I was terribly nervous about how to talk to people, so sometimes I just read what others had to say before chiming in and sharing my thoughts on whatever topics were being discussed. I highly encourage this. Unfortunately, many people continue this behavior for so long that it becomes a type of crutch—particularly on networks like Facebook. These people are called "lurkers." Lurkers go online only to see what everybody else is doing and only rarely share what's going on in their own lives. And as a result, lurking can sometimes get them in trouble.

Habitual lurkers have become the modern equivalent of what used to be known as neighborhood gossips. "Did you hear about Susie Jones? She and her husband . . ." well, you know how it goes from there. Two bad things can happen to those who lurk for a little too long: 1) you might find yourself at a party where you know everything about what happened lately with so-and-so—who shares online—and end up in the awkward position of sounding like a stalker, or 2) you might find yourself being ridiculed by others who figure out that you only lurk because you start talking in person about someone else and sounding like a gossip. It's fine to troll Facebook, but, if you do, let people know you're there. It takes a fraction of a second to hit the "Like" button. Then you acknowledge you saw that a friend went on a vacation or that her daughter graduated from high school.

Sharing can be done in many ways. You can poke fun at yourself, you can talk about bumps in the road, you can be light. If you don't want to be serious about everything or positive about everything in your life, that's totally fine. Results from some studies are now coming out that say reading everybody else's good news online all the time can make some people feel down about themselves, so don't just share the rosy stuff. It's okay to share the ups *and* the downs. And if you're grateful about something, show it.

Sharing online has actually helped me embrace the concept of gratitude more outwardly. If you pray or meditate, you know what that means—taking a moment to be grateful for the meaningful things in your life. Some people also show that gratitude online. It's a form of journaling. People tag their posts on various social media sites with the keyword "grateful" or the hashtag #gratitude. As an experiment, type either of those into the search box of your favorite social network and see what you find that you might like to share with others. Sharing should be fun, and it should always be comfortable. If you find it to be uncomfortable, take a step back and rethink what—and why—you're sharing before continuing along that path.

Controlling Access

Computers and devices connected to the Internet work with a series of access controls, telling who can access what, from where, and when. Passwords and keys grant us access to certain places on the Internet. It's all a part of how we get around and how we know that our information is safe. When you log into an account on a social network, you are authenticated as one specific user, and you only have permission to do what that user is allowed to do. You can change your privacy settings from there, but no one else except network administrators can do that for you—unless you give someone else access. So this is the base level when using social networks, just as it is with using an office computer or an iPhone.

Once you gain access, you then control how others access your information. For administrators, there are commands that allow us to change who can access that data. You can decide if you want a certain folder of images to be public or private or just seen by a subset of people. That's the beauty of access controls. We can argue all we want about whether things like e-mail should be private or not, but the reality is that the architecture dictates that there are always ways to obtain access, so there will always be ways for hackers to get into our accounts. This is why strong, unique passwords, changed every few months, are recommended for any networks where you store or share important information.

Building Your Digital Persona

Some of us already have digital personas. When we do that vanity search, we find a few—or more—results about us. For others who are newer online, you have the opportunity to create your persona. Then there's a third category of those who wish to alter their digital personas or create secondary personas, for a variety of reasons. If your profession or part of your life has changed—say you were a baker and you're now becoming a rocket scientist, or you were married and you're now getting divorced—then you might want to alter your online persona to reflect the changes in your life. It can take a lot of time, but it will be worth it in the long run. There are various ways of doing this, but I recommend creating a project plan with goals, just like you should do when creating a completely new online persona. This can also work if you're creating an anonymous or pseudonymous persona. It takes time and attention to detail. You have to go back to all of the images and information you have listed online and decide what you want to keep as a part of your online persona moving forward.

Some people maintain two different online personas or even a variety of different social media accounts for different interests. This is worth considering if you have two widely different careers or if you juggle interests that tend to have conflicting audiences. I have one friend who is a realtor and a filmmaker. Those two careers do not often intersect, so she has created two individual profiles, and she keeps both of them updated on a regular basis. I first began blogging about a wide range of things on my own personal blog—from politics to figure skating—but I soon learned that there were very few people who wanted to read about both.

When I started blogging about figure skating for BlogHer (for fun since I had been a competitive figure skater several years ago), I opted to create a different BlogHer profile, separate from where I blogged about politics. And I created a Twitter profile—@segsk8—dedicated to figure skating. I don't tweet there often, but it allows me to hop back into figure skating conversation online when there are major competitions, and that way I don't lose followers on my other accounts where they don't care who landed a triple Lutz that day.

Sometimes it makes sense to create separate profiles for different vocations or activities. Most people do this simply, like sharing different Pinterest boards. Some people opt to create entirely different online personas to keep their work and home lives separate. I recommend putting a lot of thought into this before you make that kind of major change because it can come with unintended consequences, like losing touch with important friends in your life if you end up only updating one of your online personas. The best thing I can recommend when it comes to updating your digital persona is to not completely close old accounts. You can tell people that you are moving—say in the case of Twitter, where people will more often change their usernames or switch to new accounts—but you should not completely delete accounts for a year or more, until you are absolutely certain you're ready to move on. Once that information's gone, you can't get it back.

Clout vs. Klout—Real Online Influence

I almost winced at writing this section because the term "online influence" has become so overused in the past few years, but the concept has taken root and will remain an important aspect of how social media is viewed over time. Influencer networks and individual online influencers can wield a lot of power when it comes to brands and campaigns. Companies court people they consider influencers based on their digital footprints—numbers of followers, blog comments, overall digital reputations—and engage with them to increase their own traffic or sales. If you follow celebrities on social networks, you know they are another type of online influencer. It can be easy to become starstruck online if an influencer retweets you, replies to you, or follows you. I recommend against spending too much time on this, however, because it's generally not worth the effort.

In reality, influence is in the eye of the beholder. I advise not becoming tied to numbers or rankings or scores on influence charts or when viewing social network followers. In the end, these are just numbers, and they don't say anything about who you are as a person—only how you rank on one metric created by someone else.

And any system of metrics used to rank online influence can generally be gamed, so there will always be people out there who game the system. If you use social media for business, it might be worth knowing what your Kred and Klout scores are. Kred and Klout are two systems that analyze your social media usage and following. They give scores based on their algorithm-based analysis, but I recommend not being too attached to whether those scores go up or down. No automated system can fully grasp your actual credibility with others. It's better to pay attention to general trends in social media than to get too deep in the weeds. Keep abreast of your real digital clout—who engages with you regularly and how your profile is generally seen online—not just numbers of followers and friends.

Find people online who *you* feel are worthwhile and interesting. That's what matters. Most of us have people in our lives who influence us or mentor us in one way or another, and those people may or may not spend much time online. Putting influence in a personal perspective allows for a deeper understanding of what the concept can mean to each of us. In my experience, the quality of digital content and relationships far outweighs quantity. Your best friend may have five followers, but she's your best friend, so she holds more real influence in your life than some actor you've never met. It's all relative, and much of it is subjective, so you can use influence metrics as general guides, but I wouldn't bet the farm.

Reputation Management

For anyone who works in a public space, takes on high-profile projects, or works with a large audience, your online footprint can be a necessary part of operating online. Most of us just worry about maintaining a positive reputation and not having our identities stolen. Rather than worrying too much about online reputation, think about carefully curating your own information online and controlling how public or private that information becomes. We all have reputations—online and off—whether they only exist in small neighborhoods or whether they span globally. The key is to control your content, stay aware of how others perceive you online, and make sure to correct problems if they arise.

Take for example if you have a common name, like Jane Smith, and a blogger wrote a post about another Jane Smith who shoplifted, using your photo from the Internet. Your friends might think you shoplifted. You would need to get in touch with the blogger immediately to let him or her know about their error. If you take care of these things from the beginning, it becomes less likely that you need to worry about fixing entries online about you that may look negative. In the event, however, that something negative about you is published on a blog and it can't be removed, there are companies like Reputation Defender that can help. Setting up search alerts and running regular vanity searches keeps you abreast of what's being said (or shown) about you online and helps prevent these kinds of problems.

TIPS AND TAKEAWAYS: .YOU

In order to get the best sense of how you want to present yourself online—how to build the best possible .YOU—remember these important tips:

- Develop a big-picture vision of who you are offline and what you want to reflect online, including whether or not you need more than one digital persona.

- Pick a place to call home online for the primary location of your digital identity—a website, blog, or social media page you can call your own.

- Draft a succinct profile summary about yourself, and select an appropriate profile photo.

- Create and share digital content that reflects the authentic you—this is what will build a positive reputation and online influence over time.

- Optimize your content for search engines, and secure your access through passwords and privacy controls.

- Remember that you control your digital identity through the creation and management of all kinds of online content—text, images, audio, and video.

CHAPTER TWO

FRIENDING IS TRENDING

 "Friends don't let friends do stupid things—alone."
—Unknown

The Internet is full of memes mocking people for doing and saying ridiculous things online—and it's true, a lot of that happens. But in my experience, most of what happens on social media comes from a more genuine, friendly origin. Most people like to share with each other and help each other. We like making friends, and we like keeping them. We're social creatures, and social media has accelerated our abilities to communicate for a wide range of reasons.

In 2009, my friend Roxane felt like her world was crumbling down. Diagnosed with an incurable lung condition, her doctors were about to place her on a transplant list. In a panic, she posted to her friends on Facebook about her situation. "Doctors can't figure it out," she wrote. By chance, one of her friends from high school saw her post. As an East Coast doctor, he knew of some other tests that could possibly identify Roxane's condition. Lucky for her, one of the new tests identified the issue, and she was able to undergo treatment, stay off the transplant list, and become healthy. When asked about the experience, Roxane says, "Facebook saved my life!" In short, the combination of her own initiative, her lasting friendships, and modern technology rescued her.

Follower Friendly

Friendships take many forms, so it's safe to assume digital friendships reflect that diversity. Functionally speaking, that means we see a wide range of activities, insights, and media shared by our friends online. What each network calls a friend may differ, but that's just terminology. Some social networks allocate "friends" to users; others focus on "followers." Facebook, for example, has both. The difference typically is that friends are people who are mutually connected, who would like to read each other's content online. Followers are people who just follow your content, people who you don't necessarily consider close friends. Twitter uses the term "follower," but you can follow someone back regardless of whether they are a friend or not. Learning the different styles of etiquette on the social networks you visit can help you to keep from making mistakes down the road.

The term "follower" can be a little confusing. Some social networks use it because it reflects the technical architecture behind the software. If you're following someone on Twitter, for example, that means you selected his or her "feed" (posts, as published) as one to show up in your account. If they follow you back, they will see your account in their regular stream or timeline. If they don't follow you, they can still read your feed; it just means they have to visit it specifically. It doesn't necessarily mean they don't like you. Now that Facebook, LinkedIn, and Google Plus, as well as the visual networks like YouTube, Instagram, and Pinterest have all adopted the "following" lingo, you can pretty much follow anyone unless their account is totally private, in which case they just want to have followers they know and trust.

Each social network has a unique focus. Facebook and Path, for example, both place emphasis on friendships. Most other social networks use the term "follower," and some just go with connections. In the case where you're using a social network to genuinely keep in touch with friends, I recommend that you only accept as "friends" people you have actually met in person or have had some sort of conversation with in real life. This helps maintain safety and privacy as well as intimacy.

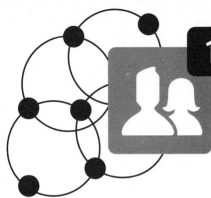

150,000,000,000

There are *150 billion* friend connections on Facebook.

For example, my friend Cynthia, mentioned in Chapter One, is a Facebook friend, a LinkedIn contact (since we've worked together in the past), and a Twitter follower. Each of those relationships is mutually exclusive yet part of the same online conversation. If I want to see what she and her kids are doing, I'll more likely find that on Facebook. If I want to see what she's thinking about education policy, I'll check her Twitter feed. If I want to know what organization(s) she's currently affiliated with, I'll check her LinkedIn profile. When I want to get in touch with her privately, I can send her an e-mail message, text her cell phone, send her a Twitter direct message, send her a private message on Facebook, invite her to a Google Plus hangout, Skype her, etc. I have several options, but I usually stick to e-mail for most friends unless I happen to have seen them on a particular social network within the past ten minutes.

Where Everybody Knows Your Name— Finding Your Friends

If you can't find a friend either by searching your old information or by asking other friends, try an old-fashioned search, but think strategically. You can search the names of friends with Google or Bing, but you also want to provide some other information to narrow it down— there are a lot of John Joneses in the world. So try a city you know that he lived in, or a sport he played, or, perhaps if you're lucky enough to remember his wife's name, enter that too. The right piece of information can dramatically narrow search results.

You can also search directly within social networks like Facebook and LinkedIn. (Note: Most web search tools work better than the mobile versions.) Think also about alumni networks or organizations where they might be a member. You can look people up through those sites as well. Finally, you can find people through your friends without even asking for their help. Just search their friends on Facebook or through whatever your primary social network is. If you're already connected there, you can more quickly identify people you may have forgotten to add to your network.

Once you're connected with friends online and the numbers reach into the hundreds, it is useful to find ways of categorizing and organizing them if you want to engage more specifically. Say you have a book club, and you want to be able to contact all of the members at once. Social networks allow you to group your friends—Google Plus has circles for this, and Facebook has lists—and this can come in handy. I find organizing my friends geographically to be extremely helpful, for example. If I need a new doctor in my area or have a question about a local restaurant, I can post to my local friends list. If I'm traveling back to Kansas City for a visit, I can put up a post for all of my KC friends to let them know I'll be in the area. If I want to talk about a social-media-specific topic, I can post to people who are on my social-media-professionals list. I consider this a favor to the rest of my friends because it doesn't inundate them with content they might find uninteresting. So categorizing can have some great uses.

It can get tricky when you're dealing with acquaintances vs. friends vs. colleagues vs. family, so some social networks have come up with ways of dealing with this. Shasta Nelson, founder and CEO of GirlfriendCircles.com, defines circles of friendship that I find very helpful—online and off: "Contact Friends, Common Friends, Confirmed Friends, Community Friends and Committed Friends." She also defines five circles of intimacy: "Curiosity, Exploratory, Familiarity, Vulnerability, Frientimacy." Frientimacy is the circle where your closest friends reside. So if you're using a network like Facebook, the friends you designate in your "Close Friends" group would be your Committed Friends with whom you feel that sense of what Shasta calls "frientimacy." Those are the friends you contact regularly and trust with your feelings, concerns, and experiences.

Sharing Is Caring

Sharing online really does begin with caring. We want to see what's going on with the people we like and love, so we turn to social media. Friendships encompass all kinds of activities and emotions, but, at the core, we want to keep in touch. We share various parts of our lives so that our friends get a glimpse of what's going on—the good and the bad. While you can keep tabs on friends on any social network, the etiquette of each network differs slightly, so those that cater most to friendships make it easiest to share in an inclusive, friendly way.

Friendship, of course, is also about having fun and sharing that fun with your friends. Path, a small social network intended just for close friends, is a great place to do that. My friend Katya Obukhova travels all over the world for her work, and she posts photos on Path, Instagram, and Facebook to share her journey. I love it because I am able to share in her joy and see her smiling face in some amazing locations.

Some Privacy, Please

Most of us enjoy sharing with friends online, but we don't always want to share everything with everybody. Privacy settings exist for this very reason. Sometimes it's okay to share publicly—tweets of interesting articles, photos at events, news announcements—but, in my experience, most people don't want the rest of what they share in social media to be public. There are varying degrees of how private people choose to be. As a result, I generally advise people to err on the conservative side and to default their postings to private (just approved friends) unless they have a specific reason they want to have public communications for their work or outside activities.

Unfortunately the onus is on us to ensure our posts are kept private. Facebook previously had all posts defaulting to private, meaning they were only shared with friends. Now they're defaulted to public. Many people don't realize that. Social networks can do this sort of thing, and you have to pay attention or your content will become public without your knowledge. Every day for the first few months after that change, I saw more friends on Facebook who posted something that came up as public—usually a photograph with their kids—and I often followed-up privately with a note explaining the change so they could change their privacy settings back. Most people don't want photos of their children posted publicly—or at least not too often. It's best if we assume this about others and ask for their permission before posting or tagging any photos of them or their kids. My friend Beth Blecherman, known as "Tech Mama" online, shared something that Randi Zuckerberg (sister of Facebook's Mark Zuckerberg and author of *Dot Complicated*) tweeted: "Digital etiquette: always ask permission before posting a (Facebook) friend's photo publicly. It's not about privacy settings, it's about human decency."

Beyond that, just keep it smart and considerate. And remember there's a time and a place for everything. If someone posts something on your public wall or even where only a subset of friends can see it, you should have a set of guidelines you consider to help you decide whether or not what they have posted makes you comfortable. Facebook allows you to configure your settings so that you must approve anything that other people post on your Timeline—like with blog comments. That way, if someone writes on my wall, "Great seeing you last night at Jane's party," and I didn't want all of my friends to know I was there, I can hide that post or decline it. Always think about how many people you want to be able to see posts on your social media pages, sites, profiles, timelines—whatever they're called on each network. For any space that is yours, make sure you know what's being placed there, just as you'd think about what you post elsewhere.

Complimentary Commentary

I remember well the first time I received a comment on a blog post. The comment was from someone I'd never met, and I felt lucky to have someone even read my post, let alone comment on it. But it didn't take me long to figure out that I had started a conversation. Sure, the post was an experience I felt like sharing, but I realized the true benefit of blogging came from the interactive part of the process. This was before social networks like Facebook and Twitter existed, so most people didn't have an outlet for public writing or sharing with friends beyond e-mail. I had written articles that were published in print or online, but the comment format was markedly different. Suddenly, I wanted to know what my readers thought, not just whether or not they were reading my work. We connected and bonded over a conversation-like experience—much more personal than I'd had through one-way publishing.

It is worth noting that we can become too dependent upon our online communities, and I see that happening much more in younger generations where the kids grow up knowing they can source their friends any time for ideas and information. Personally, I've found that engaging through blogs and social networks to solicit ideas, feedback, or input can be incredibly helpful. Still, some people can get hung up on receiving likes, replies, comments, or favorites on their posts on social media. Pavlov knew, as we all do, that we become conditioned for favorable social engagement and praise. But with social media, we face social nuance and technical details. For example, it makes no sense to be upset if nobody is commenting on an important observation you posted at 4:00 AM. By the time other people are awake, they have plenty of other things to read and they may not see your post. Everything we post online is subject to timing, algorithms, and whims of users. Self-esteem is too important to leave to these devices.

Good Notes—Rewarding Positive Behavior

My daughter's kindergarten teacher used what she called "good notes" to reward positive behavior. If the kids did a good job and stayed out of trouble—by not being too silly or unruly during class each day—they went home with a small yellow note, about the size of a note card, that said they had a good day. It was a real source of pride for the kids and an important statement to those around them. If they were not good, they went home empty-handed. The absence of the reward was enough to remind them to try harder the next day. One bad day wasn't a big deal, but repeated transgressions meant missing out on bigger prizes, and that seemed like a travesty to the five-year-olds.

The Internet is a giant playground full of opportunities for good notes. When you play well with others, follow the rules, and say nice things, people usually respond in kind, and you have a great time. If you aren't so good—meaning that you don't play well with others—you come out of the experience with nothing to show for it. You're not necessarily punished by negative comments or hateful e-mail that some may fear, but you're ignored, left alone, and eventually ostracized. Take time for common courtesy. Don't blow people off. It just takes a few seconds to write a message back that says "thank you." Some people think they can say things to others online that they shouldn't or couldn't say to their face. For the most part, this is wrong and is the root of many mistakes.

Small errors are easily forgiven because there's a certain acceptance for newbies who goof up at the beginning, but continued transgressions can cause problems. Just like in a kindergarten classroom, you have to choose whether you want to play nice—or not. Sometimes I call the Internet the "wild, wired West" because it can seem lawless without much policing; in reality, it's more like a neighborhood-watch area where communities protect their residents. And don't be fooled into thinking it's like Las Vegas—contrarily, what happens online spreads like wildfire, especially if it's juicy.

Unfriending and Unfollowing

At some point, you will notice you have either been unfriended or unfollowed on one or more social networks. My advice here: Don't track who does this, and don't take it personally. People leave social networks for all kinds of reasons—perhaps they don't use it enough or they decide they don't like certain features—and sometimes people unfriend or unfollow by mistake. I purposely don't keep track of how many Facebook friends I have, and I never set up any programs to watch who unfollows or unfriends me, so I don't get caught up in the psychological mess of worrying about these things. It's not healthy.

If you notice that someone is no longer connected with you and it troubles you, the best thing you can do is leave it alone. If it keeps bothering you, just drop them a line casually and say you noticed they weren't your Facebook friend any more and take the high road. Did you do anything to upset them? Did you do something by mistake that led to the unfriending? Maybe it was an error. Maybe he or she decided to spend less time online and deleted the social media account. Your online "friendship" is not always a direct reflection of your real friendship. If she unfollowed you on Twitter, maybe she just decided she already sees your posts on Facebook, or maybe she felt you tweet more often than she wants to read. Each person uses social media a little differently, just like each person manages her home differently. Your best friend's house might be a little messier than yours; that doesn't mean you love her any less.

Over-Sharing in the World of TMI

There's a reason an acronym exists for Too Much Information (TMI). You know that woman you avoid because she always tells you way too many details about her latest medical encounter, like her recent root canal? Sometimes she does it online too. So it's important to find a happy medium online that keeps your friends informed yet not overwhelmed. It requires some finesse, and trial and error, but, overall, follow the basic rules of etiquette offline and you'll be fine. For example, would you want a photo of you looking silly and drinking with a friend to be published in the local newspaper? No? Then I recommend not posting it online. E-mail it privately to your friend if you want her to see it. Don't blast it out for the universe to view. Because once it's out there, it's fair game forever.

Think about what you do when you have friends over to your house. They may notice photos you have on your bookshelf, or perhaps they see an item that jogs a memory from a particular time. That prompts conversation about events or activities, and builds new memories. Friends like to share memories—whether they're from summer camp long ago, or from a more recent baseball game. It's important to share these things. That's what's expected in social media, and it's perfectly fine. One photo, one memory, one conversation. Simple and clear. Of course, if you're engaging with family members about that same event, it may be different—you can e-mail several photos to the grandparents so they can save them, print them, whatever. Just cater to your audience the way you would if you had guests in your home.

Introducing Emoticons

The first time a friend wrote me a message with a colon parenthesis like this— :) —I didn't know what it meant. It took me a while to figure out it was supposed to be a smiley face. I had gone long form before that—in the early days of the Internet—making more detailed faces like this:

Most people don't have the time or inclination to do things like that, nor do they need to these days thanks to the invention of graphic emoticons. Emotional icons like :) and :(come in handy. Emoticons come pre-installed on the iPhone, so now any time I send text messages, I can use them. That allows me to express emotion virtually through text messaging when I can't send photos or connect directly via video or in person. So if someone sends me sad news, I can reply with a sad face along with a kind note. It can be very helpful especially for sensitive people. Words can have multiple meanings, and, depending on how you use punctuation and wording, the recipient on the other end can wonder what you really meant to say.

While it may seem like we only share our activities online, we share our feelings quite a bit. Since technology is inherently neutral, sharing feelings in a way that truly conveys what we're feeling can be an art form. Emoticons were developed as a way to show emotions like you would in person, with representative faces. It may look like a cheat to some people, but, for others, it's become part of their regular digital parlance. Whatever you choose, conveying genuine emotion is the key. Sarcasm and subtle feelings can be easily misconstrued in text, so tread cautiously.

Earlier this year, *Real Simple* magazine launched "Get Real on the Internet Week." They asked readers to share what they were really going through—not just the sugar-coated version. And it was great. I hope they repeat it in the future. Some experts say that social media can create strain in people's lives because it seems like everyone is having successes every day—when that's not reality. Most social networks are set up so that only positives are acknowledged. Say you post "It's our anniversary!" about you and your husband, with a cute photo of you two on your wedding day. Of course people will "like" it or +1 it or favorite it.

But what happens when you post that your pet died? Anyone who wants to send condolences has to use the comments because there's no "bummer" button. Designers don't want to put in a "dislike" feature because the conversation can become toxic when opinions are put into play. Some social networks have been experimenting with "I feel for you"–type buttons, like the "I feel . . ." feature now available in Facebook as an option for posting along with text or images. This allows for empathy in negative or sad situations. But for now, most social media emphasizes the positive, which means that anything negative going on in your life becomes trickier to share, if you wish to do so. As social media evolves, I expect we'll see more options for sharing a wide range of emotions. If you find yourself becoming confused, go back to the basics. Remember your audience and what they want to see from you online.

Worst Practices—
How to Lose Friends Online

Everybody screws up sometime, and mistakes can be particularly obvious online. Here's a list of common errors:

- Ranting or posting polarizing remarks. If you have a controversial opinion, find a forum where it's safe to discuss, or keep it offline.

- Personal attacks. Sometimes they're called "flame wars." Don't directly accuse anyone of anything online, call anybody names, bully anybody, or otherwise verbally abuse anyone.

- Graphic photos. There are some photos that should not be posted online, such as photos of dead people or suffering animals. Don't post a photo your followers might find disturbing.

- Sexist or racist material. Don't post tasteless, rude, or offensive remarks about a given gender or race online. Take an extra five seconds to consider whether the material might offend.

- Whining. If you're sad or upset, say so, but don't drone on.

- Oversharing. Roger Cohen called oversharing one of the "great scourges of the modern world" in his op-ed "Thanks for Not Sharing" in *The New York Times* in 2013.

- Overposting. Most social networks run on an etiquette that assumes people will post one to three times per day if they are active users. Less often is fine. More often tends to annoy people.

- Mundane noninformation. "I ate toast this morning." Thrilling. Save it for the dog.

- Bad linking. Make sure the links you share are genuine—particularly on public networks like Twitter. You don't want to reshare links that contain viruses or send people to bad websites.

- Overt narcissism. One of the reasons social media gets a bad rap stems from people who post continually about themselves, including seemingly endless "selfies," or photos of themselves, and very little about the other people in their lives.

Correcting Mistakes Online

Most etiquette mishaps that occur online happen by accident and tend to be minor. On a rare occasion, someone will offend and lose a friend. I certainly hope that doesn't happen to you. In general, we're lucky that the digital era is still in its infancy and most people forgive easily. I find that most mistakes wouldn't have occurred if people had asked a couple of simple questions: 1) Would I say this to a crowded room full of people? 2) Would I say this to someone's face at a party? If the answer to both of these questions is yes, then you can generally go ahead. You still may make mistakes, but that's how we learn.

Sometimes we hit the "Send" button before we realize what we've done, and then whatever thing we didn't mean to write or post is out there. Or we post something thinking maybe it'll be okay, and, five minutes later, we regret doing it. Now what? If you do this, the best thing to do is own up to it quickly, then remove whatever you posted. Say, "I'm sorry. I didn't mean that. I'm removing it." Then remove it, and, if anybody has a problem with it, take it to a private forum—talk about the error in a personal message, or pick up the phone to correct the problem one-on-one. Don't let it fester if somebody gets upset.

If your friend makes an error and you find yourself trying to explain to him or her what she or he did, then the best thing to do is resort to basic etiquette and kindness. Assume it was an error, or at least pretend to assume it was an error, and tell your friend, "Hey, I assume you meant to do this instead," or, "Just FYI, you may want to consider removing that post—it could offend someone." Another tactic to use is "Hey, I think this is funny, but there's one part of it that somebody else may find upsetting. . . ." Just remember to be nonthreatening and calm throughout the process. Give your friend a hint that it's not cool and that you'll forgive her little mistake, but make it clear that other people may not be as forgiving, so she should fix the problem before it escalates.

I heard a sad story from a friend who unfortunately became engaged in a heated religious debate on Facebook. One person posted his particular view on an issue, and my friend replied with a view slightly contrary to his, thinking that after five years of friendship and participation in the same religious community, he would listen and they would have a productive discussion. My friend stated her view diplomatically, and she was then lobbed with insults by those who were participating in the conversation. She didn't intend to offend anyone; her friends should probably not have posted their opinions in that forum. Essentially, they unknowingly set a trap, and she fell into it. They didn't actually want a conversation; they were upset and they posted in anger, and she, in her attempt to be helpful, lost out on friendships with people who had been in her life on a regular basis. She resorted to unfriending them on Facebook. To my knowledge, they never apologized for the position they put her in or for insulting her.

In that case, you can argue that the friendship may have inevitably been doomed, but I think they made the basic mistake of saying something online that most people would never say in person. After their argument, they should have apologized and worked to repair the relationship. This leads to another problem: the digital apology. The digital apology has become the victim of modern-day casual culture and lazy lingo. Expressing sincere apologies can be very difficult online. Through a combination of fear and laziness, we can now simply say "sorry" via text or private message, and many people think that's enough. Often, it's not.

The omission of a pronoun (and a verb) alone connotes a lack of sincerity, like a kid reluctantly apologizing without wanting to do so. I'm tired of these kinds of disingenuous remarks. Sure, it's better than nothing, but a real apology includes the word "I" and gives some detail. If it's done online, it should be at least a few sentences: "I am so sorry that I said that—I didn't realize it would offend anyone, and I removed the statement immediately. I sincerely hope it didn't hurt your feelings. That's the last thing I would want to do." This kind of apology can go a long way. It would be better, of course, to pick up the phone if possible and go right to the source, providing auditory sincerity so the offended person understands it's a real apology. But in the digital age, we don't always have phone numbers handy or other ways of contacting people that we engage with online, so a direct, sincere note is often the best way to respond in these cases.

If You've Got the Social Media Jitters

Does going online ever make you anxious? You're not alone. It's like feeling nervous about going to a party where you might know some people, but mostly you're just friends with the hostess. She says something and you laugh, and someone else reacts negatively, and it prompts you to become anxious. The same thing can happen when your friend posts on her profile or timeline and friends comment. Except when you're online, you're looking at several friends' timelines, in essence party-hopping from friend to friend within the course of a few minutes. You see more friends online on Facebook in ten minutes than you would in person in a month, in most cases. What can you do?

Shasta Nelson emphasizes that we should not shy away from social media; instead, we should think about the source of the anxiety:

A lot of psychologists and sociologists are saying social media is to blame for this anxiety. I really feel that online tools can be excellent for our friendships. Every tool has its limitations, like Facebook. A few women have said to me that they hate Facebook because of the social anxiety element, but I definitely don't. We all go to dinner parties where we're prone to be comparing ourselves to each other. If you're insecure about your life, you're going to be insecure whether you're online or offline—whether it's at Facebook or a dinner party.

Big Days Online— Announcing Major Milestones

Milestones have been a public relations key for ages. It's the anniversary of the third time the fourth president's best friend's dog jumped through a hoop—let's issue a press release! That's how social media feels sometimes when we share milestones, but, joking aside, people usually only share milestones when they think they're a big deal. I shared the milestone of finishing the first draft of this book because it felt huge to me—writing all of these pages. I took a picture of the printed manuscript and posted it on Facebook, and I was surprised that more than 200 of my friends took the time to "like" the image. It was just a milestone to me personally, but, because my friends are on this journey with me, it made them happy too, which then encouraged me to share other personal and professional milestones in the future. That's how we support each other as friends online.

Birthdays in particular are a big deal on social media. A lot of kind people will come out of the woodwork just to send you a nice birthday note on Facebook, and it feels good. Virginia Hefferman put it well in her 2011 *New York Times* opinion piece: "Yes, Facebook can be capricious and tyrannical and tedious, but the leviathan social network is the best thing that's ever happened to birthdays." It doesn't matter whether you've only signed into Facebook once or whether you use it daily. On your birthday, you'll hear from people regardless.

Friendship IRL (In Real Life)

During the process of researching, writing, and editing this book, I constantly reached out to my social network for stories and thoughts on various topics. I like to call it friend-sourcing because this process was much more personal to me than blindly sourcing the crowd. On some days I purposefully curated whom I asked questions, while on others I threw a line to my entire personal community to see who would bite. I was so amazed and humbled by the stories friends shared with me, knowing that their stories might help others learn more about the beauty of digital life.

When I reached out on Facebook seeking personal stories about digital friendship, I received all kinds of stories from friends from different parts of my life—high school and college classmates, professional colleagues, acquaintances who share hobbies, parents of my daughter's friends—who shared a variety of examples showing how digital media had helped them. One friend told me about how her mother lost power during Hurricane Sandy and how she reached out online to find someone to help her mother take care of her pets. Immediately a Facebook friend who wasn't much more than an acquaintance offered to take in her mother's pets and cared for them until her power was restored. Another friend shared that she wasn't able to qualify to cosign a loan for her daughter to attend her dream college and had posted her experience on Facebook. It turned out that a friend there (again, an acquaintance) had founded an organization to provide loans and scholarships to LGBT families. He offered to cosign the loan, and her daughter now attends NYU.

In truth, we will never know how digital friendships can impact our lives unless we put ourselves out there. I consider digital friendships one giant opportunity to pay it forward. You never know what you may encounter each day when you log onto your favorite social network or check your e-mail. You never know who might come into your life or bring you joy. But one thing's for certain: as technology continues to play a greater role in our lives, we have more and more opportunities to reach out and help others online, and to make our own lives more meaningful in the process.

TIPS AND TAKEAWAYS: Friending Is Trending

- Find and connect with your friends apart from public followers.
- Consider the circles of connectedness to help guide you to group friends online.
- Share only whatever is comfortable to you, and be careful not to overshare.
- Don't get hung up on comments and "likes."
- If you make a social error online, fix it immediately and make sure your apology is genuine.
- Pay it forward online.
- When in doubt, take your friendships offline and go back to the basics—friends are too important to leave solely to technology.

CHAPTER THREE

LOVE IN THE TIME OF MESSAGING

 "If love is the answer, could you please rephrase the question?"
—Lily Tomlin, American actor and writer

My digital life began just before my dating life, so it's no surprise the two quickly became entwined. I met my first boyfriend thanks to the early days of the Internet, and nearly every subsequent romantic relationship I was part of included some form of communicating online—either via e-mail, chat rooms, instant messaging, and/or text messaging. My husband and I still reminisce about flirting virtually via Zephyr, the online messaging system we had on campus at the University of Michigan.

In the case of my first boyfriend, we met online on a BBS and then in person at a group social event. The relationship evolved from there, usually chatting one-on-one late at night on one of our BBSes. (Either I would call his computer with mine, via modem, or vice versa.) Chatting on the BBS meant using a tool similar to instant messaging or Facebook messaging, where we could type messages back-and-forth, having a conversation by typing rather than talking. I remember distinctly the mystique I felt while waiting to see if he would connect with my computer each night. Sure, we used the phone too, but I think we were both more comfortable typing messages to each other. Somehow it felt like we could share more that way—I was less scared of expressing my thoughts and feelings through the written word than the spoken word.

With the boyfriends that followed, we met in person and quickly began conversing online and by phone to become better acquainted. Personally, I liked the variety of options for communicating rather than sitting around waiting for a phone call, which I think is part of the reason today's digital natives correspond so much via typed messages. The quietness of it can make it seem much more personal and private. In retrospect, I think the combination of meeting in person and online early in dating relationships can provide an ideal opportunity to get to know the other person better in a relaxed environment.

It takes time to learn what to say, what not to say, and how to say it online when you're dating and communicating in a romantic situation, but taking the time to develop these skills is well worth the effort. The tools may change, but the general ideas stay the same: words, images, and sounds express feelings. Navigating romantic relationships in a virtual environment handicaps us in some ways and endows us in others, so it's always best to tread cautiously. Opportunities abound for finding love, nurturing relationships, and expanding horizons online.

There's no substitute for an in-person connection with a loved one, but, in the absence of that, much can be communicated online. The tools of the digital age provide us with great opportunities to connect in different ways—sometimes to our benefit and other times to our detriment. Either way, we grow and learn from our experiences. Sharing our thoughts, emotions, and experiences in different ways can enrich our personal relationships with others, romantic or not. We share differently online, so that sharing allows for a greater depth to our understanding of others in our lives.

Romantic (Sub)Text

Many people go online searching for love or to connect with someone in a romantic relationship, and, in that process, they fail to realize the role that words, images, and sound play in our interpretation of romantic concepts and gestures. It's easy to assume that communicating online is somehow as sufficient as offline when it's not. The critical thing to remember when embarking on romantic relationships online is that all three of these components matter in addition to the obvious in-person physical connection. While we have a wide range of options for getting to know people better and deepening connections, it's important not just to rely on one method of communication, or inevitably messages, context, and nuance will be lost. It may seem like we have it easy communicating online now with video chat tools, instant messaging, and texting at our disposal, but, in truth, love is difficult to find and keep regardless of the medium.

Rachel Sarah, a former single mom and author of *Single Mom Seeking: Play Dates, Blind Dates, and Other Dispatches from the Dating World,* says that online dating can feel eerily deceptive because all of the communicating you do before you actually meet—via e-mail messages, IMing, video chats, etc.—can make you feel like you really know someone. It can also give you the confidence to open up easier than you would, say, if you'd met that same guy at a bar for the first time. But more often than not, many or all of those preconceived notions you had about Mr. Dream Date go out the window when you actually meet in person.

We see many examples of online dating that make it seem daunting and scary, and then we see that one example that makes it seem easy and worthwhile. So which is it? A little of both. It's easy to find examples of highly embarrassing, challenging, and even insulting experiences online. In late 2013, Kyle Ayers, a New York comedian who happened to be hanging out on his apartment building's rooftop, live-tweeted a couple's argument and assumed breakup, unbeknownst to them. The hashtag: #roofbreakup. Even our private mistakes can now be made public online. When in doubt, take your relationship discussions offline—far, far offline.

Entering the Online Dating Domain

When I first started researching the current state of online dating, I was surprised how many of my Facebook friends told me, "I met my husband online." Nearly two dozen of my friends met their significant others through online dating. Many of those people married and have been together now for more than ten years. Some met through online dating sites; others met on message boards or other online communities where they shared similar interests. So don't feel like you need to join Match.com. If Twitter is the social media site you love most, see who you're connected with there and strike up a conversation. You never know where it will lead. Go where you feel most comfortable. I had one friend who told me she always liked Craigslist "because I can tell a lot about people by the way they write . . . it sort of forces you to remove visuals from the process and learn about a person first. That's how I met my life partner."

Online dating has become a giant market, with resources spanning from old-school personal ads on Craigslist to high-end virtual matchmaking consultants. The average person tends to use resources that fall somewhere in the middle, putting profiles up at sites like Match.com, checking there weekly, and listing herself as single on Facebook, clearing the way for the world to allow prospective partners to find her. While most people still meet life partners through mutual friends, "one in six new marriages is the result of meetings on Internet dating sites," according to Nick Paumgarten's 2011 feature in *The New Yorker*, "Looking for Someone."

Although computer-based matchmaking algorithms first came about in 1964, online dating didn't become mainstream until around 2005. These days, it's just as natural as meeting someone through a mutual friend or at a bar. "For many people in their twenties, Internet dating is no less natural a way to meet than the night-club-bathroom line," wrote Paumgarten. "The obvious advantage of online dating is that it provides a wider pool of possibility and choice." The other advantage: math and science. These sites make money, not only from advertisements and volume of visitors, but also from successful complicated algorithms. Match.com in particular prides itself on being the expert in understanding profile data and system usage to refine their system.

Online Dating Sites

The range of online dating options has grown to include so many different types of sites, it can be difficult to determine where to begin. To make it a little easier, I've separated that world into categories.

- Mainstream online dating sites (most of these are fee-based): Match.com, Chemistry.com, eHarmony, OkCupid, HowAboutWe

- Blended sites (communities that have a dating component): MeetMe, SeniorFriendFinder (for seniors)

- Younger, edgier sites: Plenty of Fish (free), Nerve, Tinder (an app)

- Mature dating: Meetcha (over 40), OurTime (over 50), MatureSinglesOnly

- Gay & lesbian dating (LGBTQ): Gay.com (men dating men), Dattch (for gay or bisexual women), Match.com and OkCupid (both have preferences for women seeking women, etc.)

- Religious-based: ChristianMingle (Christian), J Date (Jewish), LDS LinkUp (LDS/Mormon community with a dating component)

- Political: BlueStateDate (Democrats), RedStateDate (Republicans)

- Online classifieds: Craigslist, newspaper-based online sites

- Location-based: SinglesAroundMe, Hinge

Stranger Danger—Privacy and Digital Dating

It is important to decide how public you want to be with online dating. Any profile(s) you create should reflect the amount of privacy you would like to have during the process. I advise erring on the side of more private to begin with, particularly in regard to name and location. You can always open up to people more once you chat with them and do background searches. Better to go this route than to end up with unwanted stalkers—or more likely, a barrage of ugly spam. Think about how private or public you want to be during the process before you sign up for any sites. Think also about what you post and how that could be construed.

I heard one story of a man who opted to go with the username "craziefox," as in "crazy like a fox," on dating sites where he was looking to meet women. His alias was interpreted by some of the male users as a female username, so he received several unwanted advances from other men. This is not uncommon. A recent article in Jezebel tells about a male Reddit user, OKCThrowaway22221, who pretended to be a woman on an online dating site, thinking he could do this as an experiment for a few days and see what it was like. He set up his profile, and, within minutes, he began receiving messages from men. Here are a few things he wrote about his experience:

> Guys were full-on spamming my inbox with multiple messages before I could reply . . . They would become hostile when I told them I wasn't interested in sex. Seemingly nice dudes in quite esteemed careers asking me to hook up and asking me to send them naked pics of myself . . . I would be lying if I said it didn't get to me. Within a two-hour span, it got me really down and I was feeling really uncomfortable with everything . . . I ended up deleting my profile at the end of two hours and went about the rest of my night with a very bad taste in my mouth.

If anyone is ever rude or mean to you on these sites, if someone bullies you or uses sexist language, note that all of these dating sites have blocking capabilities. You can block the offender easily, usually with one click, and you'll never see or hear from him or her again. Use that feature. It can be your best friend. In the late 1980s, I used to get crank phone calls from boys and men about once or twice a week, and the only way to avoid them was to hang up and hope they would eventually go away so I wouldn't have to change my number (which I did, twice, before I turned eighteen). E-mail addresses are somewhat like phone numbers of late, but we have more control and can block people or exile their messages to spam folders. These tools are essential while dating online.

Dating review sites have become popular in recent years. Lulu, a mobile app for women only, allows women a safe space to review men

How to Choose the Best Profile Photos

Choosing a good profile photo is always important, but it's especially so for online dating. Here are a few standard rules for photo selection and editing when building online profiles:

- Start with recent photos. Anything more than two years old doesn't represent your current appearance.

- Select a photo where you are well lit, sensibly attired (nothing too revealing), and wearing some color (so that you don't look washed out), and not wearing sunglasses.

- Make sure you are the only person in the photo (and if you crop someone else out, make sure no part of that person is visible in the new image).

- If you don't have a good photo in your existing collection, ask someone to take a photo of you (with today's smartphone technology, you should be able to get a good shot and put it online in a timely manner).

- When cropping, try to stick to standard sizes—rectangles or squares. That makes it easy for most applications to import the image.

- Don't attempt to use Photoshop or do any major touch-ups beyond red-eye reduction unless you are experienced with that type of photo editing, or you will make your photo look like you are hiding something.

- Choose a photo that shows you smiling.

We've all seen offenders. I heard one story of a man who used his driver's license photo for his online dating profile—he took a photo of the photo and posted that on the site. With the software and mobile devices we have available today, there's no excuse for that kind of laziness.

they have dated. This has pros and cons. A dating review site can warn women about a dangerous or abusive man, but it can be a problem if a woman writes something vindictive—but not true—because she feels burned. Imagine that guy trying to date again. What if his new girlfriend shows him what his ex wrote? Remember the tenet: Don't put anything online you wouldn't want to see in a local newspaper. Be ready to stand by anything you post on this type of site.

This leads me to the general warning: Never share your home address until you have already done a background check on the person you're conversing with online and after you have met him or her in a public place. This may sound extreme, but I've heard some awful stories. Predators come in all shapes and forms; we all know they are online. Usually the people you meet are not vicious or abusive—they may be odd or rude, but not dangerous. Still, it is always important to stay safe and do your homework. Google is your friend. Use what you already know about people you're meeting to dig up additional information on them before getting together in person. There are also services that can do background checks—some of them are automated through online dating sites. Use them. That's why they're there. My friend Larisa noted, "It's amazing how much information can be found when someone uses the same username and [photos] across multiple types of sites . . . an ounce of prevention and foresight beats a pound of cure and a restraining order!"

Your Screen Name Matters

According to *Love @ First Click, The Ultimate Guide to Online Dating*, by Laurie Davis, choosing the right screen name, photo, and profile description are the three most important steps in the initial online dating process. "This is your opportunity to be uniquely you and generate interest in others to meet you," Davis says.

First contact with a prospective date can be exciting. Most of the online dating systems are similar to Facebook, Twitter, MySpace, and other social networks in that they have a private messaging system for connecting users directly. These first "e-mail flirtations," as Davis calls them, are important to attract attention, qualify yourself, and begin a conversation after you've connected with a potential match on the site. In order to find the right match, be authentic, and remember to use appropriate language when meeting someone new. This means being more formal than casual because politeness goes a long way. There are plenty of impolite people online, so set yourself apart there first. Davis also advises avoiding sexual conversations before meeting a person for an actual date—otherwise, it may lead to a situation where sex is all the person expects. After you meet someone online, there's a window of opportunity you have to connect in person and see if you hit it off romantically. If you meet too soon, you could put yourself at risk of wasting your time; if you meet after too long, you risk building up all kinds of assumptions and expectations about your date.

We now have so many options when it comes to dating online that some people are beginning to wonder if all of these choices actually could do a disservice to the dating pool. In an *Atlantic* article called "A Million First Dates," the author asks, "Does the plethora of available single people online make online dating so easy there's no reason to work hard to challenge real-world relationships?" The author goes on to make a great point: "No one knows exactly how many partnerships are undermined by the allure of the Internet dating pool." There is a trend, noted by Dan Slater, who authored *Love in the Time of Algorithms*, that suggests that "the rise of online dating will mean an overall decrease in commitment." On the flip side, he wrote, "Internet dating has helped people of all ages realize that there's no need to settle for a mediocre relationship," and that's a good thing.

This may mean some people raise their standards while searching for relationships online. It may also mean that other people lower their standards, figuring they can find anything and everything online. Because anything and everything is so easy to find online—including various forms of pornography—those in search of casual sex can find it much more easily today than ever before. If that's what you seek, you will find it. I'll cover this further in Chapter Four: The Kids Are Online, and what this is doing to the sexualization of teens and young adults.

E-Flirting 0101

Once the flirtation advances and you're comfortable with the person you're dating online, chatting through e-mail, texts, Skype, etc., can be extremely fun. It's a great feeling when you connect with another

I DO!

1 in 6

new marriages is the result of meetings on Internet dating sites.

person and you share a kind of chemistry around ideas, emotions, and attraction. Turning that into a deeper relationship can take days, weeks, months, or years, but my advice is to enjoy the ride. I look back now at all of the fascinating conversations I had online with people I dated from age fourteen through my late twenties (when I became serious with my future husband), and most of my memories are happy ones of staying up late at night and typing messages back and forth about music, physics, philosophy, and life in general.

I recently posted the question "What does online dating mean to you?" on my Facebook page. My favorite response? "It means . . . *Thank goodness* because I met my prince charming online and we were married a week ago today," my friend Kathy said about meeting her husband Jeff on eHarmony. Their courtship began in June of 2011, when they began e-mailing, texting, and chatting by phone before meeting in person that October. They became engaged one year later and were married the following June.

My friend Melissa shared with me the story of how she met her husband online. This is a fairly classic online dating story, but it took place a decade ago:

> We met on Nerve.com when it was a tiny site. I heard about it from a college friend. Bars aren't my thing, so I posted a profile. I did not include my pic, but offered to e-mail it. When a few guys e-mailed, I always met in public, on a transit route. I never gave

my home phone, only work. Daniel and I chatted via e-mail a few times, then agreed to meet for a drink at a wine bar. We met again for dinner before I gave him my home number. I did google him to see what I could find out. He'd told me where he worked, so I searched there first. The name and photo matched, which put me at ease. Then we sort of went from there . . . it was kind of awkward in 2002 to say you met online; it was considered so backwater. But now people think it is adorable.

Melissa and her husband were ahead of the curve in the world of online dating, but she already had figured out how to be safe and smart during the process. Once she crossed the threshold of becoming comfortable with her date, that made the rest of the experience much easier, online and off.

What's Your Relationship Status?

At some point, many of the people in our lives enter into long-term relationships. When they decide they're ready to tell the world about that commitment, digital media now provides a way for them to do that. Facebook provides a variety of options for designating our romantic relationships. Other sites have more nebulous or generic notations, like "Spouse/Partner." It's always your choice whether to participate in this type of semi-public announcement of your relationship, and that of course brings with it new challenges, like ensuring you and your partner are on the same page, sometimes literally, making that announcement. Engagements and wedding announcements, in particular, elicit a wide range of online feedback from friends, so you have to be ready for that when you take a big step.

I'm now a forty-year-old suburbanite, so most of my friends these days are already married or in committed relationships. It's common for me to see them post anniversary photos or messages to their spouse/partner about how happy they are together, sharing special milestones online. That's one of the best parts of sharing your friends'

Cranking the Heat with Digital Smoke Signals

If you're in a committed relationship and want to engage with your partner online, it's wonderful to be able to share meaningful experiences that way. Managing long-term romantic relationships online requires a little finesse and a lot of concentration. When the match is right, and when in-person communication is the primary method of working out problems, generally the online component isn't a problem, but there can always be errors. Let me reiterate that, in case you missed it. You'll make mistakes if you're not careful.

It's so easy to write something online and have it be misconstrued. If you can, focus on keeping online communications genuine and comfortable. Be respectful, thoughtful, and creative, so your partner knows you're there for him or her. Often we communicate so quickly online in our busy lives that it's easy to make the (often incorrect) assumption that our partner isn't interested in talking because he or she is really just too busy. That's where emoticons and shortcuts can come in handy. Learning to communicate well online isn't just important for romantic relationships—it's important for all relationships.

When in doubt, if there's a sensitive topic, find a way to discuss it in person, or in the most fully communicative medium you can, so the other person can see what you're going through and detect intonation and emotion through your voice and facial expressions. If those are missing, it's easy to make all kinds of assumptions that can easily be wrong, causing rifts in relationships that aren't easily repaired. Keeping up good communications—including sending loving messages—with your partner online in all kinds of forms will help you grow together and individually.

The web also has a wide range of resources for couples online. One popular dating site, howaboutwe.com, has turned to the relationships side and built a second business based on finding great dating experiences for couples. It's a paid subscription that includes daily deals for couples, a nice concept. Other online lifestyle, travel, and culture sites often have romantic date ideas for readers and members, so check them out. You never know what you'll find until you look.

Twenty years after our first Zephyr flirtations, my husband and I still communicate daily via text message and e-mail and emoticons—even when we're in the house just a few rooms apart. I think a lot of modern couples are moving in this direction. Thanks to digital media, we all now have more ways to keep the romance alive when we're in partly virtual relationships. The joke my husband and I like to make is that we talk to each other more by phone when he's traveling. When we're both home, we communicate either in person or via text message because that's what works best for our busy lifestyles as parents and professionals.

lives online, in my view. It's like being at their wedding reception all over again and enjoying their happiness along with them. I think it's wonderful when couples share photos of their big moments together, like my friend Julie Peters and her husband did.

Julie had an intimate wedding and reception and shared the photos online for friends who couldn't be there with her, and I felt much more connected with her because she was willing to take the time to share photos from the event with us. Our parents were close friends for many years, so it was wonderful for me to see photos of her dad walking her down the aisle. These moments can be so powerful and personal to share, and we now have a unique opportunity that no one in history had before us—to share the entire experience with others far away. One friend of mine even webcast her entire ceremony online!

If You've Changed Your Name

Since the occasion for changing one's name is more likely to happen in conjunction with marriage than with most other activities, I wanted to note here what happens to your online identity if you change your name. Luckily, sites like Facebook allow for you to keep your maiden name, and that helps with their search algorithms. If someone wants to find you, it's still easy enough. If you change your last name completely on other sites—LinkedIn, for example—not only could you confuse work acquaintances who don't know you recently married, but you could also confuse search tools that will not be able to connect links of your old name to links of your new name. Essentially, you're creating a completely new online identity, no different than if you created a pseudonym or decided to go online anonymously.

Clearly, if you don't like what's online about you, this could be positive. In my case, one of the reasons I didn't change my last name was because I had already been published so much online under my maiden name. Half of my online footprint would have been split off. This is fine for most people, and usually you can keep your usernames on sites and still change your name, but when it comes to search engines, they only look for keywords. They have no way of connecting that Jane Jones is now Jane Johnson. Just something to think about if you are contemplating changing your name in the near future, and it's something that the next generation of young women online will face when they marry and look into changing their names.

When Virtual Rejection Is Real

Sometimes, it's difficult to get rid of someone who expresses interest in dating you. I've experienced my share of this, in a variety of forms, and it's always uncomfortable in one way or another. How to say no to people can differ in any situation. Some people can't take subtle hints like avoidance or telling them "I'm busy," so you have to be straight with them and say you're not interested. Others won't accept that and will keep pursuing you further. I think it's always good to be clear about what you want and what you don't want, but online, it's difficult for people to figure out what that means. Sometimes, a well-written e-mail message helps clarify your thoughts if you're not interested. Other times, a phone call is more appropriate. Sometimes neither works well and you have to just give the person time to absorb what you've been trying to say.

In one case, a friend of mine told me about a man she had dated for a year. He seemed uninterested in making any kind of long-term commitment, but he kept contacting her. Finally, she decided he couldn't take a hint, so she came up with what I thought was a rather creative solution. She registered the domain name callmewhenyoureserious-john.com (I've inserted John here, but I don't actually know what his name was), she put up a basic web site that pretty much said the same thing, and she sent him the link the next time he reached out to her. It worked. She hasn't heard from him since.

The Kinky Side of Digital Life

"Are you into bdsm, Goddess?" This was a real message someone sent to an acquaintance of mine who was using an online dating site. The author's attempt to get my acquaintance interested missed the mark, but the point was well taken. She wasn't inclined to go there. It should be no surprise that there are people online who are into all kinds of different sexual practices, and there are also a wide variety of social networks for people who are interested in nontraditional relationships like polyamory or various types of fetishes.

If you tread into those worlds, just be aware that anything you do should be kept as anonymous as possible—even a web search of one of those networks can be logged on your computer or on a browser. Nothing is truly secret. There can be some positive aspects to open sex communities online—there is for example a significant group of sex bloggers and "naked bloggers," who blog about sex and cover sex-related topics online, helping to teach others. Sex education is important, but, again, tread cautiously. Anything you read or view online—pornography or otherwise—can potentially be logged and discovered by others.

Once you move into more involved sexual relationships online, you can come across all kinds of information and images. It has become much too commonplace for men to take photos of their genitalia and send them to women. Some subcultures where casual sex correlates with social status encourage people to take photos and videos of themselves naked or doing sexual acts. When I began dabbling in modeling in college, my model trainer gave one piece of advice to me and all of the women and girls she was coaching: If you take your clothes off for money, you won't ever be able to put them on again. What that meant was, even if it pays more to be photographed in lingerie, for example, your photograph will always be out in public, and you will always be remembered for being a lingerie model.

The same concept exists online, as everything is now a news medium. If you e-mail a topless photo of yourself to your boyfriend, he may post it or share it with others. He may use it against you after you break up. There are countless possibilities. The same thing goes for sex tapes or any kind of online video. In one case where a woman showed herself half naked to a man on Skype, assuming her image could not be shared, he took a screen shot of her and was able to then forward it to others. Be safe, be smart.

Breaking Up Basics

It's all wine and roses in any new relationship, but, when it comes to an end and much has been shared online, it can be as difficult to split online as it is offline. Divorces can be particularly hairy online. In some cases, it can be even worse before the official split. I heard of one case where a husband actually posted on his wife's Facebook page asking her forgiveness for his transgression. This I would most definitely not recommend making public. It's a private matter. Keep it that way. Conversely, one story someone shared with me (anonymously, of course) featured a woman who found out about her husband's affair because a friend of hers posted a photo of him with another woman. I'm not going to pass judgment on what may or may not have happened in real life here; these are just anecdotes to show what can happen in relationships online today. Keeping relationships private is very difficult.

When it comes to major breakups or divorces, most people leave that information off social networks, opting instead to share privately with close friends via e-mail at the beginning; however, some people who live online and use social networks extensively will opt to share that information virtually. In many cases, it can't actually be avoided. If you have selected in Facebook that you're married to someone, you and/or your spouse have to determine at what point you will terminate that "official" relationship. It may happen before you separate legally, after you move out, or after you've signed the divorce paperwork. That's an individual decision, but if one person decides to disconnect the "married to . . ." status on a social network before the other is ready, the deed is done, and both parties will have to deal with it online, as well as off.

If a split is mutual and both people can be amicable about how they share that information, their friends can assist them in making them more comfortable with the transition online. Remember that whenever your status changes from "Married" or "In a relationship" to "Single," some of your friends will undoubtedly notice. To your friends, it looks as if both people altered their Facebook pages when a relationship ends. It's not obvious who initiated the split. In reality, one person generally makes that decision. You'll need to be prepared for the messages that will come to you from friends asking what happened, when you broke up, and how you're doing.

In the amicable breakups, it's easier to manage because both people involved can stay friends online, their friends can stay friends, time passes, and the dust settles, even if it's occasionally awkward when they see each other in person. It's nearly impossible to completely avoid seeing your exes online, however, even if you block them on every social network. You still might see photos of them with mutual friends or see articles retweeted, etc. . . . It's like living in a small town. You will always run into them somewhere.

With every breakup, there's a time when thoughts of an ex can provoke negative or painful reactions. This can happen as easily online as offline, and without any warning. When this happens, it's a good time to take a break from the Internet or to take conversations to a more private level with comforting friends. Anything posted online is fair game in a courtroom. Painful events happen, and it's nearly impossible to avoid them completely, but minimizing the opportunities can be helpful for the healing process. It's common to fall into depression after a breakup, and it's common to hear about the "online dating blues," when people who have tried online dating fail at starting new relationships. They feel despondent and tired of the process. This can happen to anyone offline, so there's no reason to think that online dating is somehow immune.

There are some positives that can come from online breakups. I heard about one divorced couple that—thanks to online scheduling tools—rarely have to see each other in person, even though they share parenting responsibilities. "E-mail and texting alone have practically revolutionized post-divorce family relationships," according to Pamela Paul, who wrote "Kramer.com vs. Kramer.com" for *The New York Times*. It's also important to keep in mind the opportunities that digital and mobile tools can provide for the post-breakup relationship.

What's the Future of Digital Relationships?

An acquaintance of mine, Gretchen Curtis, posted a photo on Instagram around Valentine's Day of heart-shaped cookies in Silicon Valley that had "Skype Me" written in frosting. I thought it was an amusing cultural observation. While she may have been making a joke in her caption "Only in Silicon Valley," online relationships have become mainstream. If you communicate online in your life, your romantic relationships will undoubtedly also have a component of online correspondence.

Here's one exchange I'll never forget: "I'll shoot you an e-mail," a woman said, as she grabbed her bag to deplane. The man she was speaking to stayed behind to lift his bags out of the overhead bin with a noticeable grin on his face. I witnessed this encounter one day while waiting to get off a plane. I don't remember where I was going to or coming from, but I remember the brief, flirtatious conversation I witnessed, and I wrote down what was said. Here's the thing—this is the follow-up these days. It's now all about texting and messaging.

Nobody makes phone calls any more. Some people like this; others disparage it. One of my friends wrote on her Facebook page, "call me, don't text, to ask me out on a date!" She then went on to call this behavior a result of "social media laziness." Does it degrade relationships? I think it depends on the person. Since I grew up online, I have always felt that the written word—whether delivered on the computer or iPhone—was just as good a flirtation as a handwritten note or a phone call. The trick is to experiment, have fun, and find what works best for you and your partner.

Reconnecting and Revisiting Digital Romance

We've all heard stories of people whose relationship didn't work out at one point, but then they reconnected later on and it did. In the past, when people broke up and moved apart, reconnecting only happened by chance, through mutual friends, or with someone purposefully tracking down their former love interest. Thanks to digital media, this has become much easier. We can stay casual "friends" on Facebook or keep connected on LinkedIn. Then if/when the time is right, the conversation begins again.

That's how one of my college boyfriends reconnected with me. We met in 1993 in college at the University of Michigan, we dated in 1994, he graduated and moved to Chicago, and we broke up. I graduated and moved to California, and then in 2000, he e-mailed me. I almost deleted the message, thinking it was spam, and then realized it looked like a familiar username. I opened it up, and there he was, working just a few blocks from where I was living in San Francisco. We met up and slowly became friends again. Six months later, we were back together. Now he's my husband, we've been married ten years, and we just passed the mark of first meeting twenty years ago. Sometimes I wonder what would have happened if I hadn't opened that e-mail message, but I'm sure glad I did!

My friend Anne-Marie Fowler shared the following story that I think sums up the beauty of reconnecting online and how it relates back to relationships:

> The other day, I heard a name on a conference call that I had not heard in years. It was of a man I'd known in my twenties in D.C. I recalled the last conversation I'd had with him before I moved west to San Francisco to attend grad school and work in banking. That was almost seventeen years ago. He had wanted my advice. He'd asked me how to say something to a woman who was very important to him. They were dating, and he wanted to tell her that she wasn't just another girlfriend. He was both joyful and distraught.
>
> I said, "Just tell her." He was afraid he'd scare her away. "Maybe you won't," I said. I remember wondering why he was asking me for relationship guidance. But I also felt honored that he was. I could tell he was sincere. I told him to go for it.
>
> I moved away, and we lost touch. I forgot about the conversation, for a time. Earlier this year, his name came up in some D.C. press, around his work on some piece of legislation, discussed on a confer-

ence call. But when I heard the name, that wasn't my focus. Remembering the time he asked for my help, I wondered, "Whatever happened with that girl?" In another era, I might never have known.

I searched for him on Facebook. A banner photo came up. With a guy that looked just like him. Heavier, balder, older. But smiling hugely. With three beautiful children, and a lovely wife. The same girl.

TIPS AND TAKEAWAYS:

Love in the Time of Messaging

- We all need words, images, and sounds to communicate well, particularly in romantic relationships.
- It takes time and practice to learn to communicate romantically online.
- We now have more options available than ever to meet prospective partners online.
- Communicating by text—whether in e-mail, messaging software, or text messaging—can be a great way to get to know a prospective or current partner better.
- Make sure you and your partner are both ready to make any official relationship status changes online.
- When in doubt, take it offline.

CHAPTER FOUR

THE KIDS ARE ONLINE

 "Children must be taught how to think, not what to think."
—Margaret Mead, American anthropologist and author

One day last year, I bumped into a mom blogger friend of mine who looked distraught. She launched into a hurried explanation about how her twelve-year-old daughter was texting some "boy friend" (not to be confused with a *boyfriend*, she said) throughout the day and that their last phone bill was outrageous. When my friend sat her young teenager down to talk, her daughter demanded a bigger data plan for her cell phone. "It's not healthy!" my friend cried.

She was experiencing a family crisis, triggered by her teen's need for constant connectedness. This mom's visible frustration signaled to me the cultural shift we witness every day as younger generations grow up online. Today's digital natives face immensely more complex challenges than I did at their age, but the origins are the same. By age two, toddlers can play simple games on iPhones and iPads. You blink, and your tween is texting the kid up the street about a play date. This might be the most perilous part of life online—teaching the next generation how to tread cautiously, carefully, and diligently in the digital universe. We hear so many stories of online bullies, predators, and the like, it's enough to make any parent want to egress and become a

Luddite. I'll show you what you need to know about your kids online and provide you with important resources so you never feel alone.

Baby's First Digital Footprint

As a result of my digital experience at a young age, I thought about my daughter's online footprint before she was born. When I began blogging about parenting, one of the first things I learned from other bloggers was that it's an individual choice whether to post photographs or details about one's children. I had written vague information about my experience and some of what I was going through as a mother, but I purposely opted not to post many photos. As my daughter grew, I became stricter about what I posted about her, knowing that she would have her own online footprint soon enough. This is an individual choice, but I think it's a very important one for kids today, whose entire lives will be online, often regardless of their own choices later in life.

So much is archived now. I read an article earlier this year on TIME.com that shocked me, entitled "Finally, a Huggies Device that Lets Babies Tweet When They Pee." It's a real product—not a joke. It's being tested in Brazil. Luckily, the small wireless device doesn't actually tweet public notifications to the entire world that your kid just tinkled. It sends a private notification to your smartphone, but it literally is called "TweetPee." Welcome to the future of parenting. For better or worse, technology is literally becoming embedded into all facets of our children's lives. We can keep them away from some of these technologies—by limiting screen time and avoiding embedded devices—but their external environments at school, friends' houses, and elsewhere will still provide ample opportunities for them to be exposed.

Parental Sharing Online

Like most matters of etiquette, the mistakes parents make online are often subtle. One experienced Silicon Valley mom of four told me she abhors when parents post about their children's grades. It's a personal matter, she explained, and, while parents should be proud, there's a time and a place. I guess she's seen a lot of this because she extended her distaste not only to grades but to school acceptances, advising that parents ponder how other parents whose children were not accepted might feel. These are fairly typical issues that we deal with in our lives, but sometimes it's easy to forget how large our online audience really is, and how sensitive others can be.

One mom, Jean Parks (@geekbabe on Twitter), put it this way: "My family and I discussed what [my kids] wanted shared on my blog, Facebook, and Twitter. They have veto power always." Once kids get older, they can decide what they do and don't want shared online. As I noted earlier, I opt for more privacy than less when it comes to my daughter. Now that she's older, she'll ask me, "Are you putting that online?" I'll say, "No, I'm just texting it to your grandma," or, "I just thought you were cute and wanted to take your picture." I explain what I'm doing with photos of her, so she knows. If it's something I want to put online, we have set rules about what's shareble publicly (usually just a general statement or a photo that does not include her face) or among friends (occasional photos of her doing something notable, like with her first art project of the school year). It's all about building trust with your children. If they trust you and you trust them, then you can always talk about what's going on online and have a dialogue about it. If you remember not to embarrass them, remember how fragile social networks can be at their age, and realize how important things are to them (vs. just to you), that's a big first step.

It's important to think about what to say about your kids online—*before* you post something. Do you post photos at parties? Do you share big family milestones online? Do you let others know where you are? Geolocation—the ability for your devices to tell where you are at any given time—is both a blessing and a concern for kids. These are personal decisions, but I recommend erring on the side of privacy at first. It's easier to become more public with the information you share. It's not so easy to change what you've already posted online to become private later on. In fact, it's very difficult, and, in some cases, it's impossible. There's also the TMI department—how much information is too much? Does everyone want to know your kid is sitting on the toilet trying to poop? Not really. This is just one example. Some people post about potty training, but I personally won't go that far.

Let's Get Organized— Family Management Tools

As my daughter got older and I began scheduling activities for her, I learned how convenient it is to organize family-related projects online. Finding good childcare, previously the bane of my existence, has now been addressed through digital media. When my daughter was a baby, the only resource I had for babysitters was the local parents club e-mail list. I used local temporary nanny agencies, but they were not very good and often charged a premium. Luckily, a few sites and apps evolved over the past few years, such as Sittercity, Care.com, and UrbanSitter. Both have different features and user interfaces, but they address the same problem—how to find caregivers locally. They have background-check services, recommendations, and profiles for caregivers, and they list rates and availability.

One of the sites I love that doesn't require anything from me except the time I put into it is called Cozi. It provides a suite of family tools, including elements that help with family safety and security issues as well as family time management. I personally like the family calendar. My husband and I chart all of our appointments that blend into family time, so we know when our daughter has activities, when we need childcare, when we're booked to go out, when I have events, when he has events, etc. You can access it anywhere—from your smartphone or laptop.

Many family-related applications are now going this route, with mobile apps. I can now order my daughter's school lunches online, sign her up for sports, order her school supplies, and keep informed about her activities, such as Girl Scouts and her art classes. It makes everything much easier to track and stay organized. My husband and I can communicate with our daughter's schools, camps, sports, and activity organizers. The one problem it does create, however, is the expectation that parents be checking e-mail on a regular basis. If I don't check my personal e-mail at least every other day, I might miss out on opportunities for my child.

Techie Toddlers and Precocious PreSchoolers

My friend's three-year-old daughter got a hold of her mother's Amazon account one day last year. Her mother was logged into the account. The little girl saw a Dora DVD and selected it. Due to one-click ordering, she ordered it. The DVD arrived at the house, and her parents were flabbergasted until they figured out what happened. They were lucky in comparison to some. I read about a five-year-old who spent $2500 on iPad apps in just ten minutes. He had only asked for the password to download one game, but then the system allowed him to purchase enough add-ons that he ran up a huge bill. His mother only found out about it when she received the order confirmation e-mail messages. Tip: turn off in-app purchases on any device your kids use! (You may want to disable them for yourself too.)

Most medical sources say that young children under two should not have screen time at all, and those over two years of age should keep it under two hours a day. At first, that seems simple enough. But when they get to my daughter's age, where she's exploring TV or movies, doing schoolwork on the computer, and playing games on the iPhone or iPad, the time adds up quickly. And parents can be the culprits too. According to Harris Interactive, more than 60 percent of parents have "distracted" their kids with a smartphone or tablet device. Move over, television. The cell phone is the new substitute babysitter.

Digital Natives Determined— Today's Grade-Schoolers

Giving kids some flexibility to create on computers can be empowering and educational for them. My second computer was an Amiga, known for its graphics capabilities. My dad was immediately sold on

Using Common Sense Online

Common Sense Media has become one of my favorite online resources. A nonprofit organization, they aim to provide parents and educators with information to help us make the best decisions for children on what media—online and off—they should be using, and for what purpose. They have ratings for games, educational apps, teaching resources, and family tip sheets, covering every topic from "Strategic Searching" to "Safe Online Talk." They even have a "Back-to-School Guide" that reviews applications by age level. Their goal: "improving the lives of kids and families by providing the information, education, and voice they need to thrive in a world of media and technology."

Common Sense Media also provides resources for classroom training on Internet safety. Once kids start typing, reading, and researching, the Internet is fair game for their exploration, so it's good to instill smart rules from the beginning. My daughter learned three tips: 1) Always ask first, 2) Only talk to people you know, and 3) Only go to places that are just right for you. Simple and easy to understand. Setting up proper safety systems and limits—being a part of your kids' networks online and monitoring the amount of time they spend there—can make all the difference.

This is also important: teaching young children the concepts of anonymity and pseudonyms. Anonymity can protect them, and it can protect others. I recommend using examples of these early in order to teach kids that people can pretend to be others online and why that's both good and bad. Some television shows can teach these lessons as well. I think it's interesting that the Disney TV show *Dog with a Blog* uses the concept of blogging and using the web anonymously, as have other shows where kids use the Internet either with anonymous personas or aliases.

Kids can do amazing things at young ages online if we allow them to experiment and explore safely. Letting them create art in apps can be fun. Some adult games—like card games and shape games—can also be good educational tools. Using cameras on phones should be taught with caution—what to take photos of, what not to take photos of, what to share, what not to share. I think the earlier, the better there. Digital modesty is an important concept to instill while children are young enough that they haven't been overly inundated by media imagery. It's also important to let them make some of their own mistakes when they're little so that they develop smart habits as they get older. As long as the mistakes can be contained at home and/or easily removed online, then it's good for them to get a taste of what can go wrong. There are some social networks just for kids that I've heard can be fun—Club Penguin, Webkinz, Scuttlepad. Some are free, and some require paid subscriptions, so be careful and do your research before you sign up.

Once you set up accounts for your kids to go online, set up a family e-mail account with all of these sites so that the e-mail doesn't just go to your child. Creating those web accounts lets you use the same family e-mail address and associate it with the accounts in question, so then you can easily monitor all accounts together. Beyond that, help them explore and engage. I heard about one nine-year-old blogger, a fourth grader in Maryland, who works with a company called Wide Angle Youth Media. I think the idea of allowing kids to blog is a great one, as long as it's closely monitored in a way that protects them from predators and from any possible future repercussions.

it over other computers at the time because it had a program called DeluxePaint (DPaint). I started experimenting with digital art at age fourteen and remember spending hours on that program. Thanks to the rapid progress in technology, my daughter can now use an application like that on the iPhone at a fraction of the size and cost. If we want to get her into something more advanced when she gets older, there are pen-mouse devices and many sophisticated art programs she can try on the computer.

It's amazing to see some kids—even under the age of ten—making their own videos online. Mobile applications make taking video so easy now. You do have to take care to teach your children what's appropriate to capture on video and what's not, and to make sure they don't share the videos without your permission and involvement, but kids love to share their creations. My daughter sometimes pins things from my Pinterest account with me, so I created a pin board of some of her favorite pins, and another with photos of some of her art projects. She's proud to have them online. She doesn't understand what all that means yet, but Pinterest is a nice, friendly environment where I felt like we can experiment a little together.

Teaching young kids that the Internet is a wonderful tool is important, but remember that it also can be scary for them. I remember one day last year my daughter asked me about how people could catch on fire from spray-on sunscreen, since she had heard about the recall. I explained that if the oil got too close to a flame, it could catch on fire. This confused her, so she asked if she could see photographs of what happens to people when they use the wrong kind of sunscreen. I decided I'd see if there were any PG photos on Google's image search, knowing my daughter is usually not easily disturbed by biological images. I found one photo of a safety ad that seemed fine to show her, and I reluctantly handed her my phone while we waited in a line.

Next thing I knew, she was scrolling through images on the iPhone of all kinds of sunburns. Then something interesting happened—she decided she didn't like the pictures, so she turned it off. Unwittingly, I had created a learning moment for both of us. She learned that you don't always want to look at all of the images you find online. I learned that, at age seven, she was already savvy enough to be using search tools, and I needed to start turning on mobile safety controls. I was also lucky that I didn't run into what's generally referred to as "rule 34" that day. (According to the Urban Dictionary, rule 34 is an "Internet rule that states that pornography or sexually related material exists for any conceivable subject.") As parents, our work is never done; as digital parents, we've signed on as part of the cyber police. You never know what your kid might find online.

The Best Digital Learning Tools

During a recent weekly assembly at my daughter's school, the principal decided to take a poll. She began by telling the kids, "Raise your hands if you like the after-school art program," and several hands went up. Next she said, "Raise your hands if you like the chess club," and she got the same response. When she said, "Raise your hands if you like the iPads we have in the classrooms," all hands went up, and the kids whooped and hollered. When the school first received their iPads last year, I had the privilege of seeing firsthand how the tablets can change the landscape of the learning environment for children. My daughter's classroom was given four iPads for use while the kids rotated between activities at certain times of day. As digital natives, they instinctively navigate these devices and help each other to learn new skills.

iPads and tablet devices hold huge potential for kids. The easy user interface, mixed with a medium-sized screen—not too big for kids, not too small to make it hard for their young fingers to manipulate—makes them just right. Since then, I have been blown away by the amount of educational applications for kids now available, as well as the creative ways they are designed. The nature of mobile application development requires simplicity, so it's difficult to get lost in these applications, and designers have come up with some incredibly innovative learning games.

Teachers can benefit now from online tools as well. My daughter's first-grade classroom took advantage of online tools like RazKids. Educational resources online include a myriad of websites, tools, and applications that parents, kids, and teachers can all use. Most have been designed for easy use, so beginner users can pick them up and immediately attain a benefit. I think this is one reason why home schooling is gaining popularity—it is much easier today to educate your children as a parent. Rich volumes of curricula exist online; there are numerous home schooling websites and communities so that it doesn't have to feel like a solo endeavor for parents who under-take this journey. For teachers, most curriculum organizations have related online information, and thanks to online sharing, people with their own creative ideas can share those too. I know a couple of teach-ers who use Pinterest to organize ideas for classroom projects.

As kids advance through grade school and into middle school, more homework tasks are being managed online. Kids can receive and submit assignments online, coordinate on projects with other students, and in some cases actually work on problem sets online. Khan Academy has wonderful educational learning tools for kids as they become more advanced with Science, Technology, Engineering, and Math (STEM) subjects. Now, grade-schoolers can start learning how to program computers thanks to Scratch, an MIT project. There are online physics lessons on YouTube, and all kinds of other types of online lessons.

Gaming, Here We Come

Kids start playing games on electronic devices at a very young age these days. I've heard stories about one-year-olds playing on iPhones. We let our daughter explore a couple of simple games at age two—popping virtual bubbles, making colorful designs. None of these applications connect to the Internet. They are all very simple. Pre-schoolers have more at their disposal—balloon animals, talking pets, shape matching, glitter doodles. Then, when kids get to kindergarten age, they can start playing the Pac-Man-type games of today: Plants vs. Zombies, Angry Birds, and the like. At first, I was nervous about these games, given the names, but, once I looked at them, I realized they're actually quite cute, amusing, and silly. They build fine motor skills, and they can be fun for parents to play as well.

Once kids enter grade school, gaming begins to become more complicated. There are amazing educational games out there—literally hundreds—and some more clearly develop skills than others, like Math BINGO, Hangman, and Stack the States, but most of the games have educational components. Some, like Cut the Rope, even teach physics principles. These are great because kids learn about things like pendulums and gravity. Then, as they get a little older, some games provide the option for them to play with others online. Here's where it can get tricky. I have only allowed my daughter to do this once so far, before turning eight. She played a word game online with a friend. They had a blast, but it didn't last long because each had to suggest words at different times, and they forgot to continue playing. It's hard enough to schedule playdates for kids that age, let alone organize virtual playtime.

As kids become savvier, they will begin exploring more sophisticated games, such as Minecraft. If you're a parent and you haven't heard of Minecraft by now, I suggest looking it up. Minecraft is not just a game; it's a social experience for many kids. Essentially the game is like virtual LEGOs, and kids can build all kinds of structures. In creative mode, it's just a building tool. In survival mode, characters must battle creatures invading their structures. The game can be played solo or on independent multiplayer servers. Some of these servers are run by trustworthy individuals; others are not.

If you get serious about Minecraft, I recommend either requiring your child to play solo or finding a techie neighbor or friend in your school community who will set up a server and maintain it as a safe environment for kids. Peer pressure can become a big factor, and then it's suddenly less about creating and more about competing. My friend Cynthia Liu, founder of the K12 News Network, suggests using a reward system. Her son "earns" one hour of Minecraft for every hour he works on Khan Academy. Seems fair, as long as you also monitor total screen time. You can learn a lot about Minecraft through YouTube videos, but these sometimes include rather colorful language, so it's best to check them out yourself before allowing your kids to view them with you.

Kids also typically start exploring game systems, like Xbox, Wii, and Playstation, in grade school. Luckily these systems now have ratings for their games, so it's easy to choose which games might work for kids at various ages. They are rated based on a variety of factors, including violence levels. The beginner games don't have any violence—they are typically sporting-type competition or thematic adventure. Computer games can also be explored at this age. Disney has some games for kids based on their movies. Here again, I recommend checking Common Sense Media as your resource guide: their ratings include negative concepts to beware of, like violence, sex, drugs, consumerism, and foul language, as well as positive concepts, like role models and upbeat messages.

So far, studies on how gaming affects kids at various ages have reported mixed results. Some of my kindest, gentlest friends loved playing violent video games for fun, and that didn't alter their personalities or professional success long term (in fact, a few of them became highly skilled, highly paid computer game designers.) Still, any game played too much can be detrimental to overall social development. That much we know. If things get too crazy, you can do what one dad in China did—his son was spending so much time on an online shoot-'em-up action game, he joined the game himself and hired an in-game "hit man" to take out his son's character. While his son was not amused, the point got across.

Power Users—Tweens and Teens

When I first ventured online as a nine-year-old (then considered a preteen, now a tween), it was on an Apple II+ computer through a 300 baud modem that was about 13,000 times slower than the speed of the average broadband Internet traffic in the United States today. Not many people had modems at the time, but I was able to call the local Dickinson movie theater BBS in Kansas City and see and read movie listings "online." The novelty soon wore off, and I began exploring other ways to connect online. I soon had one other friend who was ten years old who had a brand-new Apple IIe and who also had a modem. She and I called each other by modem through the phone line about once a week, connected, and typed notes back and forth, "chatting" online—not unlike modern text messaging. I took a course at a local computer store to learn typing and BASIC programming. The following summer, I attended a computer camp with my modem friend. I learned to translate my thoughts quickly through my fingers.

Now as a parent of an eight-year-old girl, I've been researching children's brain development and how it's affected by screen time—time spent in front of both televisions and computers. Looking back, I firmly believe part of my brain became wired to think as I typed. To this day, it's easier for me to translate my thoughts through typing than it is to express myself through speech. That's part of what it means to be a digital native. We're wired differently. But don't worry—that doesn't mean your kids will become socially inept—if anything, being online helped me as a natural introvert to reach out in other ways and connect with like-minded kids.

It's true that how you spend your time as a child helps develop those traits early, and the same thing is as true for sports as it is for the arts, reading, and technology. In my case, I was already spending a lot of time alone, so the computer gave me a window to be with others when I was at home, bored of playing with whatever toys I was into at the time. True digital natives think differently and view technology differently because it is ubiquitous in their lives. Yes, they can become dependent upon it, but not always in the ways you might think. As IdaRose Sylvester, an international technology business consultant and friend of mine told me, "The Internet, mobile, etc., are completely part of the fabric of my life; it's not some appendage or external force anymore." I certainly feel that way, and I have ever since I began making new friends online at age fourteen.

Tweens and teens learn technology and social skills at an extremely rapid pace. It's nearly impossible as parents to stay on top of everything they're doing with these tools, online and off. The best hope

Setting the Stage— Family Digital Policies

One of the best ideas I've seen for digital families is the creation and implementation of a clear, understandable policy for technology, Internet, and mobile use. Many families have a family Internet policy that evolves as the kids get older. They make purposeful decisions that all family devices stay in the main areas of the house at a charging station, where parents can monitor devices and their use. They create limits on time usage of devices. They make sure parental controls are turned on so some content is blocked. They set up monitoring tools so they can observe what their kids are doing when they are online. Some of these policies can become more specific, like the amount of screen time allowed during the week and the weekend, which devices may be used in friends' homes, rules for downloading apps, times of day for use, text limits, browsing limits, who to give e-mail addresses to, using parental controls on searches, and limiting image searches. It is important to build awareness about the risks of online chatrooms, invasive online advertising, and the process internet companies use to store personal data.

Beth Blecherman, aka Tech Mama, author of *My Parent Plan*, likes to say that "the online safety talk is the new sex talk." She explains, "One very important part of family communication is having regular talks with kids about online safety. I suggest starting online safety talks at the earliest time it is 'age' appropriate, but it is never too late." Beth also notes that family policies, contracts, or rules will need updating over time as children get older and as technology evolves. "I have been having regular talks with my oldest son about online safety for years. He knows that to keep his freedom online, he needs to share with us what he is doing online. He also knows that together as a family we will review the privacy settings and communication etiquette for each site."

Along with the idea of the family policy around using the web, mobile device use deserves special attention. Some concepts to make clear to your kids are: The parents bought the phone, the parents own the phone, the parents will always have access to everything on the phone. This sounds simple, but this could be overlooked for kids getting hand-me-down devices at a young age. I recommend reading "Gregory's iPhone Contract," a real contract written by two parents for their son. It includes some great specifics in this area. Here are a few of my favorite points:

- "Do not ever ignore a phone call if the screen reads 'Mom' or 'Dad.'"
- "Do not use this technology to lie, fool, or deceive another human being."
- "Do not text, e-mail, or say anything through this device you would not say in person."

Some other smart ideas: If the kid breaks the phone/device, the kid pays to repair or replace the device. Don't text or e-mail anything to any friends that you wouldn't want their parents to see. It's all common sense for adults when we read these tips, but we have to remember, this is all new for kids. And since Gregory was an older boy, his parents made the point that he should never view porn or send or receive any images of anyone's "private parts." Unfortunately, this has become common practice for some teens and young adults. Best to make sure that *never* happens.

we have of keeping our digital native children safe and supported is to continue a constant dialogue with them, imparting as much wisdom as we can about human nature in the process. Tweens and teens need to learn that these tools they possess hold great potential for power, and that how they use these tools can be incredibly important both in the short and long term. As parents, our rules need to take into consideration our children's digital lives.

Monitoring Kids Online

Not every parent will opt to monitor his or her kid(s) online, but most parents keep an eye on their kids in one way or another—either physically, by requiring them to use mobile devices in the same room where a parent is, or technically, by checking the browser cache or installing software that logs what the kids are doing on the computer. I read the results of one poll on CNET that stated 43 percent of parents admit they check their kids' Facebook pages every day. I'd hoped that would be a larger percentage. And remember that if you're just visiting your kid's page, she or he may not actually show you all posts. Some kids have gotten so savvy with posting that they'll create groups for "everyone but mom and dad" and post there. Make sure you know what your child is doing. It isn't just your parental responsibility; it's your legal responsibility.

Data privacy advocate Shaun Dakin told me what he does for his eleven-year-old. "Our deal is that I set up the accounts that he wants (and I agree to), and I do it in such a way that I have access to it. I tell him that I will monitor what goes on with each account." Parent and flexible workplace strategist Cali Yost put it more bluntly: "Letting kids go without checks on them online is like letting them loose in New York City." Her husband checks their children's posts daily. It's also important to realize that this isn't just about your kids' safety; it's about continually teaching your kids what's appropriate online. Sometimes they'll post a pouty face photo because their friends will think it's cute, not thinking about how it could look to a potential future employer. It's your job to explain that to them. The same thing goes for content ownership. Teaching your kids early about copyright;

who owns images, music, videos, etc.; and that they shouldn't download content without permission can be a good lesson.

Schools can run into problems as well. One parent at a local school told me that the school uses Gmail, Google Calendar, and Google Drive for classwork and homework. The products are linked and are supposedly only used for schoolwork, but, in her case, it was easy for her son to go create a YouTube and Google+ account not for school use.

Teaching Digital Etiquette

Last summer, my daughter and I received an invitation from a friend to attend a dressy luncheon at a country club. We dressed up and arrived at the luncheon on time, hostess gift in hand, displaying our best manners. As soon as we sat down with the other ladies, the two other girls who had come with their mothers whipped out iPhones. They proceeded to stay on their iPhones the rest of the luncheon. They barely said a word to anyone. I was mortified and was put in a difficult position. After teaching my daughter that it's rude to use your iPhone at the table during a meal, here she saw two older girls doing just that. There was no one else for my daughter to talk with, nothing else for her to do, so I gave up and handed her my iPhone. Sure, it allowed me to talk more freely with the other ladies at the lunch, but I felt bad for my daughter.

An interesting thing happened on the car ride home. First, my daughter didn't want to play on my iPhone in the car because she had spent so much time with it at the lunch. Second, she told me how boring it was and how she was sad she wasn't able to talk with the other girls, and how rude she thought they were for just sitting there playing the whole time. It made me happy to see she learned from this experience in a positive way vs. seeing the behavior of the other girls as an excuse to get away with the same thing in the future.

We are at a crossroads in our digital culture. As busy people and dedicated professionals, we fall easily into habits of employing mobile devices as constant companions, and we can forget that we're modeling behavior for the generations behind us. Here's what I have to say about it: Even the most powerful, most wealthy people I know—members of Congress, billionaire executives—take time off for their kids. Steve Jobs used to go home early to jump on the trampoline with his children. As parents, we know modeling good behavior is key, but it's so easy to just pull out the smartphone and look up this one thing or just check that one message . . . and it's a slippery slope that can lead to your teenager spending the entire meal staring at a device instead of talking to you, and you have no leg left to stand on when enforcing family rules.

Tiffany Shlain, filmmaker and founder of the Webby Awards, created a digital video series called "The Future Starts Here" for AOL. Her first video highlights the concept of the "Technology Shabbat":

> Every Friday, we all unplug from all of our technologies and don't turn them on again until Saturday Evening. Unplugging for a day makes time slow down and makes me feel more present with my family. I not only appreciate this quality time with them, but it has also made me appreciate technology in a whole new way. By Saturday night, we can't wait to plug back in.

I think the tech Shabbat is an excellent teaching tool for kids, not to mention the benefit it provides for adults.

How to Protect Your Identity

It broke my heart when I heard what had happened to one of our babysitters when she first started working for us. Her boyfriend had just moved to Australia, and, when she attempted to get a passport to visit him, she was denied. Why? She was eighteen years old, and someone had stolen her identity when she was a child. They found out when she was twelve, and she had been battling the legal claims since then. Six years of her teenage life were marred by this criminal's actions. And her story is sadly not unique. It's a common scam to steal social security numbers of children and use them to apply for credit cards. Luckily, it's now fairly simple to monitor your child's

92% of teens use their *real names* on social networks.

credit score online and to track any information that could relate back to her or his identity.

Two applications I use on my iPhone—and I keep them on the first screen in the top left corner—are FBI Child ID and ICE. ICE is the international acronym for "In Case of Emergency." I list my husband and my sister as ICE contacts in my phone, so if someone picks up my phone, they can find them. FBI Child ID allows parents to insert photos and identifying information about their children and have that readily available to send to law enforcement if needed. Think about what you do for emergencies now for your family and how online and mobile tools might reinforce that plan. You never know when it might make all the difference in the world.

Cozi has taken on the family safety and security issue as well, coming out with tools called Family Locator, Family Files, and Password Vault. These help track kids, store important family documents, and hold onto passwords for family accounts. Each year, more companies build apps for monitoring kids on the Internet and on mobile phones, so parents can be sure they're safe. As our children grow older and the Internet grows wiser, I expect the need for heightened safety and security applications only to increase. I'm not advocating sharing all of your personal data with these companies, but I do recommend keeping some information safe where it can be accessed in emergencies.

From Online to Offline

The first time I wanted to physically meet up with people I met online, my dad was seriously worried and protective. He insisted upon going with me to the first offline gathering of local BBS users. He met some of them, and he stayed out of my way and let me talk to them—they were mostly other teens, mostly teen boys. Back then, I could count in under a minute the number of people who were online in the whole of the metropolitan Kansas City area. The people I met were harmless, we became friends, and my dad determined he didn't need to chaperone me after that to meet my online-offline friends. Things have changed. A lot.

Now a teen's average day consists of texting friends and love interests, doing homework online at night, meeting up with friends after school, posting their activities on social networks, and any number of other communications that can potentially be traced through location-based software or device-tracking technologies. That's not to mention recent social phenomena of superfluous pouty selfies and overt sexting. In truth, most teens know what they should and shouldn't do—digital natives are well aware of the risks—but what they may not understand are the consequences. College admissions officers now view social media accounts as part of their process. It's not a game.

Teaching our kids how to watch out for strangers and other dangers used to be all about not talking to anyone they didn't know and not getting in the car with anybody unusual—rare things in the physical world. Now we can encounter thousands of strangers in the course of a minute online. It's become essential to teach teens, and even tweens, how to stay in safe environments, how to watch out for strangers or ill-meaning people online, how to deal with them if they encounter them, and how to report them. Hopefully, we won't get to the point of having to file formal complaints or change e-mail addresses, especially since we have sophisticated blocking software available to us now, but these are real dangers. There are cyberstalkers who can take their efforts offline if they're so-inclined. There are online black markets where all kinds of illegal products and services are exchanged. Even gangs have gone online. Just because your kid is under your roof doesn't mean he or she is completely safe.

Cyberbullying: Do Something About It

According to Pew Internet, 95 percent of children ages twelve to seventeen are now online. Of the teens online, 80 percent use social media sites. Supposedly 46 percent of teens go online several times a day. Social media has become a big part of older tween and teen social culture. As a result, bullying has also gone online. The bad news is cyberbullying is rampant and can cause horrible repercussions. It's becoming all too common to read stories about teens committing suicide after being bullied online. Usually there's an underlying force involved—a brutal culture at school, problems at home, teen depression, or a combination of those things—but cyberbullying is serious. Over 85 percent of teenagers have witnessed cyberbullying. It can lead to kids missing school as well as severe social anxiety and other mental health problems.

Cyberbullying comes in a variety of forms, from public bullying—mean posts on a Facebook Timeline, for example—to e-mail insults, unfriending, outing other kids, or cruel text messages. Now that kids can connect with each other in more ways than just in-person or on the phone, there are more ways they can be bullied. I've heard parents complain about Tumblr, Snapchat, Whisper, and Ask.fm. One parent told me, "Ask can get ugly. Really sexual. Mean." These sites allow for anonymous use, and teens go on there to communicate, thereby opening themselves up to potential cyberbullying. A few of the parents I talked with about Ask.fm in particular said their daughters had to delete their accounts because the environment had become so toxic for them.

It's not the apps themselves that are the inherent problem. (In fact, many of these social networks have wonderful communities—Tumblr in particular has become extremely popular.) These sites are created for people to use how they wish; unfortunately, when they can be used without identity or oversight, things can get out of hand. Laura Sydell, Digital Culture Correspondent for NPR, says,

Advanced Computer Science Education

Coding is cool. Repeat after me: *coding is cool!* We need more kids in the next generations to adopt technology for their careers. We particularly need more girls to take on technology roles. We need their ideas, their skills, and their perspectives to develop more-well-rounded hardware and software of the future. I was a lonely girl in tech—the only girl who could program a computer at my school. Now, technology has become so ubiquitous that anyone at any age can learn it, and you don't have to go enroll in an in-person course like I took to develop these skills. I still recommend that kids learn typing because it can be helpful later on for school. I don't have to look for keys on the keyboard; I instinctively know where they are. The keyboard and my brain work in combination. That is one of the best things about being a digital native.

Web design is another skill that I recommend teaching kids of all ages. It's not as technical as you may think. App development can also be taught at a young age. I mentioned Scratch earlier. It's a great tool for teaching kids programming. Then when they're in high school and college, there are options in school and online for learning every programming

"The problem is that there is always another site. For parents it's like a game of Whac-A-Mole." Damage can be done when kids feel publicly shamed or embarrassed. The number of people who see the bullying matters less than the way the kids are bullied because, as digital natives, these kids' offline and online identities have become intertwined. Some say that teens have become way too dependent upon the "hive mind," i.e., the collective thoughts and ideas from their friends, gathered through social media. The other part of the problem is that only 5 percent of teens tell their parents when they have been cyberbullied. This needs to change.

language available. There's a site called Homeschool Programming with online education for kids of all ages. I also recommend programs like Girls Who Code, Black Girls Code, Code Academy (codeacademy), and computer camps for kids.

I attended a computer camp when I was a tween, where I met other girls and boys who were excited about computer programming. I found that I wasn't the lone girl in tech, and I gained confidence. The National Girls Collaborative Project funded camp at Cerner is part of the Kansas City Power Source App Camp at the Lee's Summit High School. If they'd had something like that when I was a kid, I definitely would have signed up. And for moms who think it's too late to learn to code, au contraire! Check out Mother Coders, a new program that blends programming courses with onsite childcare so you can learn to code while your kid is next door. Not sure if your kid is right for programming? Do a quick search for online videos about learning to code. See how she responds. Or install Scratch and start playing with it when he's around. (Kids can start programming as young as seven or eight years old!) You never know where it could lead.

Luckily, we have many ways to combat cyberbullying. First and foremost, the kids now know how to identify it and crush it. When tweens and teens are educated about what cyberbullying is and why it's wrong, they protect each other, like having friends back you up on the playground. And this is the type of behavior that quells the public bullying. Second, parents can help their kids by explaining why certain sites are dangerous. You can stay on top of this if you research these topics, talk with other parents, create trust with your teen, and talk with him or her about these things on a regular basis.

Advocating to Protect Kids Online

For parents of tweens and teens, it's useful to know about COPPA, the Children's Online Privacy Protection Act. Websites must obtain parental permission to collect or share personal information of children under thirteen. This pertains to names, e-mail addresses, etc., but the devil's in the details. Companies have to know that the user is under the age of thirteen in order to make this determination. Some sites, like Facebook, aren't supposed to allow users under the age of thirteen, but many kids under that age are making accounts, providing fake birthdays. It's not like Facebook or other sites have the ability to verify the data each individual user provides, so the onus is on the parent to watch for this kind of use.

In California, a new state law is being considered (it may be law by the time this book is published) to allow minors to remove any data about them that is put on a social network. Say for example your teenager posts a provocative photo or an offensive joke on Twitter. By law, she or he would be able to remove that post from any kind of record in the system, making it like it never happened. Most children's online advocacy organizations, like Common Sense Media, support this type of law. I believe that over the next few years, we will see more state and federal legislation related to personal information online. We are still early in this process, since laws tend to lag behind the technologies.

Digital Distractions— Young Adults with Big Responsibilities

At some point, your kids will turn eighteen, leave the nest, and live on their own—online and off. As parents, we have to think about how we're preparing them for that transition. Making sure we model good behavior in the home, managing "digital distraction" and moderating their time online—as well as our own—provides a stable setting for learning and experimenting. For troubled kids, social media can be a place to obtain help. And in the worst cases, like the case of one family in San Jose, California, when their teen daughter ran away, they were able to use social media to get help from kids in the area who knew her and helped to locate her.

Teachers can be a big help too. One high school teacher I know, Amy Reilly of Eastside College Preparatory School, likes to keep in touch with her students when they graduate. She says, "Facebook allows me to maintain a connection to these kids as they transition to adulthood and I continue to contribute where I can. I can check in when they seem distraught or need advice that they don't know they need. I don't add any students until after they graduate and so it becomes symbolic to me of starting a professional/personal mentoring relationship with them. And when I've had a rough day, I am uplifted by their accomplishments."

The transition to young adulthood isn't always easy. Some things have become better thanks to technology—students going off to college can now "meet" their college roommates online before they get to school, adding to their comfort level before they arrive. But their inherent focus on their online identities does have disadvantages. "We're raising our kids to be performers," says Donna Freitas, author of *The End of Sex*, in an interview for an article in *Vanity Fair* magazine. "College kids, both male and female, also routinely rate each other's sexual performance on social media, often derisively, causing anxiety for everyone." The public-private boundaries, misunderstood or misread by the new adult's dependence upon his or her online community for validation, can lead to an unwanted online pedigree.

Knowing how much time teens and young adults spend online, some organizations have taken to digital media and mobile to help them cope. Launched early this year, the Crisis Text Line can now be reached 24/7. The service deals with all kinds of issues, from self-cutting and eating disorders to suicide attempts. Troubled teens can feel free to text whatever is bothering them, stopping or picking the conversation back up at any time. The National Dating Abuse Helpline also allows contact via text or live chat, as does the National Human Trafficking Resource Center. So while it's absolutely frightening to think about these things happening to your kids or your friends, please let the young people in your life know that these resources exist.

Their generation feels more comfortable communicating through mobile devices than via most other forms.

Growing up online, many kids have surpassed their parents in time and experience on the Internet, and they have opted, on their own, to dial down their involvement. Many teens are deciding to leave some of the more active social networks like Facebook, instead opting for more simplified apps like Instagram, sending text messages to close friends, or—gasp—actually using the phone for voice-based conversations. As digital natives, they're not as easily impressed by the latest and greatest widget as we often are, so they can be more objective. If we can do our best as parents—teaching our kids to independently evaluate sites, apps, users, and abusers online—we'll raise the next generation of digital natives to be much savvier about the ways of the world—online and off—than we are.

TIPS AND TAKEAWAYS: The Kids Are Online

- Protect your child's digital footprint and identity as early as possible.
- Introduce your kids to educational applications and learning games.
- Keep communicating with your children at all ages about their digital device and social media use—open communication is the key.
- Stay on the lookout for cyberbullying, identity theft, and other threats.
- Remember that the digital natives will always be at least one step ahead of you.
- Model positive digital etiquette through good behavior as parents.
- Teach your kids: Coding is cool!

CHAPTER FIVE

THE SENIOR MOMENT

 "I am living in the Google years. . . . When you forget something, you can whip out your iPhone and go to Google. The Senior Moment has become the Google moment, and it has a much nicer, hipper, younger, more contemporary sound, doesn't it?"
—Nora Ephron, American writer

Growing up as a techie, I became the go-to person among friends and family, who came to me with questions about hardware, software, mobile devices, and recently social media. I never know when someone will call me or e-mail me with these questions. One day a few years ago, a close friend of the family decided that was her day to start using Facebook at age 70. She called and asked me for advice. I didn't have time to help her right then, but I told her I would call her later to talk her through how to use Facebook, step-by-step. That wasn't soon enough.

As soon as she saw the photos I'd posted on my Wall—the part of my Facebook page that all of my 1200-plus Facebook "friends" could see—she began enthusiastically poking around as most people do when they first set foot on social networks. Soon enough, she posted a note on my Wall, asking when I could call her to Chat. I happened to be online, working, at the time. I thought her post was harmless, but I responded to her privately in a Facebook message, telling her I was working and that I'd call her back later or that we could use the online Chat after I was done working.

Not understanding the difference between the private message and the semi-public Wall, she wrote back on my Wall that she was going to take her ninety-five year-old mother to the doctor—including the reason why—and that she would be back at three o'clock her time. Well, I thought that was a little too much information for others to read. Not wanting my friends to see the post, I removed it from my Wall and went on with my day.

Two hours later, she returned and posted three more messages on my Wall. "I'm back. I'm online now, so you can call me and we can chat." I chuckled at the irony that she was sharing her schedule with 1200+ people so I could go offline and call her so we could come back online and chat privately on a system we're both already on at the time. I quickly sent her another private message telling her that she was posting messages on my Wall that everyone could see and that she should reply where I was writing her so that others wouldn't be flooded with that information. She wrote back on the Wall. "I'm sorry I posted on your public Wall. I didn't mean to do that. I can't find the chat window. . . ."

I finally stopped working and called her. I knew my friends wouldn't mind one accidental Wall post, but a continual stream could have ended up in my losing Facebook friends who were colleagues or otherwise less forgiving. We both felt bad about the experience, and, unfortunately, it scared her off from posting on Facebook for a while. To me, it served as a great example why new users like her need assistance when entering the wonderful world of the Web.

It can be very confusing. It takes time to learn the nuances between public and private spaces, browsers and apps, followers and friends, and often it takes assistance from someone more experienced. Most people seek advice from their peers, but seniors generally don't have extensive information technology know-how, so they lean on those of us who grew up with computers. The good news is that the seniors who venture online usually have great reasons for being there, like connecting with their kids and grandkids, so they're excited to learn new tools to help them achieve those goals. They just need guidance in how to navigate the Web and a basic understanding of social media vernacular. Most seniors also have an interest in health and medical applications, so I've included some information about those in this chapter as well.

Sixty Is the New Thirty, Online

Seniors—particularly women over sixty-five—are now one of the largest growing subsets of people online. In fact, for the first time ever, half of American seniors are online. This makes perfect sense because older people typically adopt technology late, and, in many cases, they are coming to it mainly to connect with younger people, generally their children and grandchildren, but also to connect with each other and to stay informed. I think it's excellent that so many seniors are venturing online because they have so much experience and insight to offer the rest of us. There's also new evidence that seniors who spend time online tend to adopt more healthy lifestyle choices offline due to their ability to learn about preventative behaviors. That's right—according to research, being on the Internet can actually decrease cancer risk for seniors.

Sometimes seniors can have a difficult time diving into social media. In general, seniors tend to be comfortable with e-mail, web searches, some online games, and even observing on Facebook or other networks, but that's where online engagement stalls. I want to help seniors bridge the gap, so that the lurkers can become engaged, active, and confident online participants. I'm aiming to address seniors, children of seniors, or people who work directly with seniors.

Most seniors I know grew up in the age of the typewriter, calculator, and telephone. These tools were one-to-one. Photocopiers came into popular use in the sixties and seventies, mostly in offices, as they were too expensive for home use. I still remember using ditto paper in grade school to create handouts and make copies. This took time and effort, as did learning to type on a typewriter—backspacing, lifting up the page, and applying Wite-Out to correct errors. That's how I learned to type, even though I already had a home computer. It was a rite of passage, and I still value the experience. People often ask me

Users **55-64** are the largest growing group on Twitter.

at conferences how I can live-blog and tweet so rapidly; I owe it to the rigorous typing training on traditional typewriters. The generations before me all learned to type this way, so when I think about seniors and how they view computers, mobile phones, and the software that runs on them, I think about it like learning a foreign language or a new culture.

If you're traveling to Japan, even if you know how to say a few phrases or discern the meaning of a few key symbols, you don't immediately understand all Japanese customs for gift presentation, their nuanced greetings, or the bows they use when communicating. Etiquette takes time to learn. Some seniors need patience, hand-holding, context, and time to adapt to new technologies. Seniors who have been early adopters of gadgets and technologies throughout their lives tend to adapt quickly, whereas others won't venture online until their children and/or grandchildren more or less force them to. Some completely avoid the idea altogether, and that's okay. It's important to know when you encounter one of those seniors. Bringing seniors online only works when they are ready and open to learning.

One friend of mine tweeted in frustration, "My mom is mad because stuff on the Internet is wrong." My friend was poking fun, of course, but seniors and those who are new to the Internet have no reason to think that the information online wouldn't be correct. Other seniors make assumptions about the Internet—that it's like a worthless newspaper with inaccurate stories. If you're teaching an older person how to go online, it's important to set expectations so they don't get too shocked when they discover it's not the perfect place they imagined after all.

Teaching Virtual Patience

Many of us have aging parents, like my mom, who spend more time online in an attempt to connect with us. And they ask questions constantly about where their photos are on their computer, how to download enclosures, and the like, often misunderstanding elementary concepts of how computers and websites work. If you're trying to help your parents, sometimes you end up hurting their feelings instead. It's not easy to teach technology skills to others— particularly to older generations. Engaging with elders on this subject can be emotionally draining.

If you're a senior, make sure you're already comfortable with computers and the Internet before venturing onto social media or mobile applications. If you're helping a senior learn to use the Web, first teach them basic computer use, printer use, cell phone use, and web browsing. Teach them how to compose e-mail messages, like writing letters. Once they master that, introduce them to smartphones, texting, and photos. Then I suggest showing them social networking. Even if they don't have their own smartphones, they have seen the Internet first from a one-to-one or personal-use standpoint, and it gives them time to become comfortable with the tools before venturing into a group setting.

Feeling frustrated about technology is normal—for both the teacher and the student. I met a woman the other day who said, "Sometimes I want to throw my computer out the window!" The woman next to her, on the other hand, extolled the virtues of being wired. "I love having my online life. . . . I'm the eldest of nine kids. It's opened up a whole different world with relationships with my family." This is the key for most seniors: family. Keep at it, keep working on it, and you'll get there.

According to *The Wall Street Journal* and a report from a Pew Internet 2013 study, 43 percent of American seniors (over sixty-five) use social media, up from 13 percent in 2009. That's a sizeable increase in just four years. Why? Seniors want information, they want to be connected with friends and family, and many have part-time work or community projects they engage in that benefit from their being online. Once they get online, they're hooked.

My friend Cindy Samuels, media maven whose experience spans from the early *TODAY* show to modern blogs, became hooked early on the Internet. She says, "As a parent and now as a grandparent, I haven't lived in the same city as either of my children since they left for college. For most of those years, from ICQ (instant messaging computer program) conversations then to Facebook, FaceTime, Skype, and Twitter now, we've been connected no matter where we all were." Today she lives in the same city as her kids and grandkids, but even though they see each other much more in person now, they still use online tools to communicate.

Jen Lee Reeves, a social media trainer at AARP (American Association of Retired Persons), encourages seniors to take technology classes, saying that they build confidence. AARP now provides an in-depth online Social Media Training Center with articles on how to get started using Facebook, Twitter, Google Plus, Pinterest, video, and blogs! Anyone can take advantage of their resources, but the material is targeted mainly for seniors. Jen shared the following thoughts with me on seniors online:

> There are a few personality types emerging from the fifty-plus crowd when it comes to online use. There are seniors who have no interest and will not be a part of social media. I do not feel like I have to change their minds unless they tell me they have family members who really want them to be a part of it because that's where other generations are sharing and talking.
>
> There are those who have jumped into online communities, but without any guidance about digital literacy, security, or how the content they share and post can have a long-term influence on

not only how people think of you now but how they think of you in the long run.

There's a third group who know how to use social [media] on a personal level but do not have the educational opportunities to see the power of it on a professional level. As we work later into our lives and delay retirement, the power of using the online world professionally is important.

Lessons for Beginners

If you're helping a senior learn the ropes online, I suggest reserving a few hours to get started, and plan to take breaks during the session. Start by asking, "What do you want to learn?" Ask the senior to write down questions in advance so that you understand how much time will be required. My mother and my mother-in-law both live in different cities than my husband and I, so whenever we visit either of them, we find ourselves inundated with questions that they have saved to ask us in person about their computers, printers, routers, mobile phones, software, websites, social media, and more.

If we're not careful, it can take up a huge chunk of our visit. So we try to take care of everything we can by phone either in advance or after we've returned home. When we're there, we sit down and deliberately go through anything that is urgent and must be taken care of while we're there, like repairing or replacing broken hardware. There are two of us—both skilled techies—and it can still take us several hours to update software and train our mothers on whatever they want to learn to use during that visit. For those less experienced, well, let's just say it can take a bit longer.

Here's why the time spent is well worth it. Last year, we gave my mother an iPhone and added her to our cellular plan. I gave her a tutorial on how to use the basic features, e-mail and text messaging. The next day, my daughter decided she wanted to show her grandma a few things as well. The look on my mother's face was priceless. As I watched my daughter tutor my mother, I knew we had done the right thing. Now, texting my mother—particularly when I can send group texts and include my sister on a busy work day—makes my life easier and keeps us in closer contact. The other day, she even replied to my e-mail from her new iPhone while getting her hair done! I was so proud.

My friend Annie wrote the following post one day on Facebook, which speaks for itself:

> My brother got engaged today. My poor mother probably spent the day calling people to tell them the news, only to find out that they already saw it on Facebook (my mother is not on Facebook.)

Another friend, Sam, posted a photo of a text she had sent her mom: "Mom, I sent you an e-mail." Her mom's reply: "Where? On the computer?"

We're no longer facing a generation gap as much as we are a technology gap. Once this gap has been crossed by remaining generations, we will all be interconnected.

Organizing Information

With all of the information we're absorbing each day, organizing that information can become crucial for seniors. Taking a little time to install and set up tools and systems for organization can save a lot of time later on. Although document organizing, document sharing, contact management, calendar sharing, and online collaboration tools were developed with professional use in mind, they can all be adapted for personal pursuits, which is why I wanted to cover them here. I actually tend to use these tools just as much for my personal projects as my professional ones because I know how to use them and I find it quicker to switch gears than if I were to use some sophisticated tracking software.

A few easy ways to organize files:

- Save files on your computer, organized by file folder.
- Create bookmarks to links in your browser.
- Build networks of files and links through applications like Evernote and Pearltrees that can also be used as browser plug-ins.

Then there's always the backup plan of resorting to searching either your hard drive or the Internet for something if you've forgotten where it is. I rely on the search tools in my e-mail program and on my computer all the time, since I have so many files that go back many years.

Digital Health Data—Useful at Every Age

According to Hill & Knowlton, 14 percent of Americans use tech to self-track their health, but I expect that number to grow quickly over the next few years. That can mean anything from tracking steps to tracking food intake, heart rate, medication prescriptions, supplements, or anything else. Some tools and applications (like the Fitbit) now allow you to track your sleep patterns too, integrating that data with other information to provide a picture of your general health. You can keep this data to yourself, you can opt to share it with select friends, or, if it serves a purpose you think is useful, you can share it publicly.

Tracy Russo, online community builder and digital media strategist, explains it like this:

> Combining these two new ways of living healthier is my favorite running app from Nike, which records the time, distance, and route of your runs, while giving you the option to share it with your friends via Facebook while you are running. Plug in your headphones, and as you run, anytime someone hits like on Facebook or makes a comment on the post, you hear a burst of applause come through over your music. When you finish your run, it compares your progress to past runs and gives you an aggregate of the total number of miles you have run that have been tracked by the app and a few pointers and words of encouragement. It's offline and online integration, social, and accountability all wrapped into one perfect package.

I have one Facebook friend who previously posted every day when he went to the gym and how much he ran. I'll admit that I thought it was annoying at first, but then I realized this was his way of being held

Password Primer

It's crucial to explain to seniors how important passwords are. Seniors tend to be targeted by phishing attempts and other electronic theft because of their relative inexperience online. Learning some basic practices like to delete unwanted e-mail, never to open enclosures from untrusted sources, and always to keep passwords secure, can make a big difference between digital safety and an identity-theft headache.

Choosing good passwords isn't as complicated as it sounds. For seniors, I think it's fine to just write down passwords in a notebook and stick it in a drawer near a computer. Most seniors use desktop computers, and that's an easy way to record them. For anyone who needs a more advanced system, there are password apps where you can log passwords securely in mobile devices. For most, just an ongoing list, kept in pencil, will suffice.

Here are a few pointers I made in my 2002 article in *Security Focus Online*, "The Simplest Security: A Guide to Better Password Practices":

Passwords are often the first (and possibly only) defense against intrusion. They protect personal information—information we don't want anyone and everyone to know. In our personal lives, this means financial information, health data, and private documents.

While passwords are a vital component of system security, they can be cracked or broken relatively easily. Password cracking is the process of figuring out or breaking passwords in order to gain unauthorized entrance to a system or account. It is much easier than most users would think.

What not to use as a password:
- Dictionary words
- Proper nouns, names

- Foreign words

- Dictionary words with numbers at the end

- Any numbers attached to you that are publicly available (address numbers, phone numbers)

What to use in a password:

- Longer is better (eight characters, or more if possible)

- Numbers and special characters, interspersed

- Capitalization in unusual places

- Phrases or word/symbol combinations

How to remember passwords:

- Mnemonic phrases. Example: ImuKat! (Phrase: I'm a cat!)

- First letters of memorable phrases. Example: qbfj0tld (Phrase: quick brown fox jumped over (using a zero 0) the lazy dog.)

- Something related to the site. Example: G00gzm3frnd (Phrase: Google is my friend.)

- Something with personal meaning. Example: ArbaanSw33t (Phrase: "A rose by any other name would smell as sweet.")

Passwords should be updated regularly, in a tiered respect. For example, financial passwords—online banking or investment accounts—should be changed quarterly; social media accounts can be changed annually. Del Armstrong wrote: "A good password is easy to remember, but hard to guess." Keep this in mind.

accountable to his tribe. By posting his workouts, it motivated him to keep going. Not everyone wants to go that route, but, for him, it was important for his progress, and he succeeded in losing a significant amount of weight, adopting a healthier lifestyle in general thanks to the online component of his health tracking.

In this case, I'm describing a middle-aged writer, not a twenty-something tech expert. Demographics for online engagement in health and medical apps might surprise you. For Walgreens pharmacy, for example, their median mobile customer is a forty-five-year-old woman, and their median customer from a "PC" is a fifty-two-year-old woman. To me, these statistics show that anyone at any age can adopt online tools to help in their health goals.

Medical Applications for Patient Care

Pretty soon, we'll all be going online for some part of our medical care. For my family, our daughter's vaccinations have been logged online at the doctor's office where she went as an infant and toddler. It's handy when I need to update school records; I just log on and look up the dates of the shots. Some medical facilities log visits, test results, and other information. You have to opt in to this feature, but it can be helpful. Of course, there's pushback on how much health data is stored online, and I recommend that you stay as informed as possible and be vigilant about making sure your data is being stored securely, but the benefits can be plentiful.

One friend of mine, Alix Mayer, a health and environmental blogger, put it this way:

> Having a chronic illness and being able to search for health information online has revolutionized my personal healthcare. In the late 1990s, medical doctors used to be quite condescending when I appeared to know too much about medicine during my appointments. They'd ask if I had been "reading the Internet." I'd always reply, "Yes, isn't it great that JAMA and the New England Journal of Medicine are online?" Sometimes I would pull out medical journal

articles to make my point. Now, I go to medical appointments and my new doctors ask if I'm an MD. My long-time doctors and I go back and forth informing each other, building each others' knowledge bases. It's revolutionary.

According to Beth Leeman-Markowski, MD, founder and CEO of Neurology Research Consultants, there are many pros and cons to consider when going online for medical care, for both patients and practitioners. Pros include online support groups, educational materials, and access to information regarding clinical trials. Cons include irrelevant or outdated information and inaccurately recorded physician reviews.

Risks of Misinformation

A doctor friend of mine once told me, "I went to a doctor (as a patient) and said, 'I did something that you will hate.' Her response was: 'You went on the Internet, didn't you?'" Risks of misinformation abound online. It's easy to assume symptoms apply to you, for example, when they do not fit. For people who are untrained in medicine—or even for those who are—it can be dangerous to obtain too much information. You go online to quell your fears, only to become even more confused.

Sometimes all of the effort put into online research for patients isn't as helpful as you might think. Dr. Leeman-Markowski notes:

> I feel bad when patients come to my office armed with piles of printouts from the Internet, having wasted a lot of time, energy, and trees. There is a lot of information out there, and it is sometimes hard to know where or how to focus without some initial guidance. A lot of the investigational medications discussed on the Internet are not ready for prime time yet. It is easy to pin a lot of hope on Drug X, because it worked in a certain study posted on the Internet, but my patient is not a rat or a mouse in a preclinical study.

The Future of Digital Health

With the growing influence of "Health IT" applications, conferences, articles, and the like, I envision a huge expansion of health-related tools online in the near future, particularly for mobile devices. Even now, as wearable computing devices come to general usage, we're seeing articles about possible applications such as Google Glass helping people with limited hearing navigate and communicate through the visual feedback in the device.

The future of medicine will be more like science fiction—virtual doctor's visits, mobile applications that integrate with our bodies (like AliveCor's Smartphone electrocardiogram (ECG) that logs heart rhythms using finger electrodes), surgeries prepared for and delivered through 3D modeled representations of patient tissue, and full-scale genetic models online. It begins with programs like 23andMe, where you can send a physical sample to a lab that maps your DNA and sends you information online.

The more we share, the more we learn. While that can make some feel uneasy, the benefits to collectively charting health information—at least anonymously—can provide all kinds of long-term benefits for us and for our kids. For the most part, it's your choice what you put online about your own health, but, in an age where data privacy is often a major concern, make sure to get all of the facts.

What Are the Next Steps?

If you're a senior, which type of senior are you? Do you enjoy going on Facebook to chat with family? From there, do you relax to read today's news? Or, are you more of a voyeur or lurker? Do you enjoy browsing, but not commenting or initiating conversation? I encourage all seniors to dive a little deeper. Now is the right time to get online. It's fine to be a lurker. It's more acceptable for older people to do that online. If you're willing to take the next steps, there are a few simple things you can learn (or teach) in social environments.

1) Group e-mail—This is a great tool for seniors who want to send messages to an entire group of friends. The cc field is made for that. Becoming comfortable with using that tool and replying to the group and to specific individuals can be a useful skill.

2) Facebook likes—In just one second, you can click a little button to "like" someone's post on Facebook, and you never know when that one second of action could make his or her day. Just by showing you care, it can cheer up a friend or a family member. And when you "like" an image or a post, then you also acknowledge you saw it. You're making it clear you are an active part of that person's life. You don't have to comment on posts to be engaged.

3) Group SMS (Short Message Service)—For the senior who's smartphone savvy, this is a great tool. Sending photos to all of your children and grandchildren simultaneously can be both handy and extremely fun. Of course, you want to know if everyone's on the same network or if there are text-messaging plans that can handle the group message.

The Wrong Megaphone

As I noted earlier, seniors can have difficulty grasping the difference between public and private spaces online and group vs. one-on-one communications. The one thing I will caution in any group setting for seniors is to learn how to reply to just one person vs. the whole group, in case there are things you want to just say to one person as a follow-up, and to remember to keep a conversation on the medium where it began. Say for example you start a group conversation in Facebook's Messages feature, their private chat function. Keep the conversation there, unless you designate otherwise. If you suddenly start replying to everyone by e-mail or text message, you can confuse people, and inevitably someone will miss the context of the conversation or drop out of the loop. Think of it like being at someone's house for a party. If you keep talking and leave the room, not everyone will want to follow you, and most people will be confused as to why you left.

If seniors suffer from dementia or seemingly senile behavior, these issues can manifest digitally as well. I read an article recently about a well-known senior who had tweeted something offensive to a group of people. That group distanced themselves from him, and several posts were written about how he was acting wrongfully. I viewed the situation differently. I felt this could be an occasion where an older man with slowly degenerating mental function put his nonsensical thoughts out to the room—except the room he happened to be in was Twitter. I may never know for sure, but it's possible this man was suffering from some sort of mental confusion. We face a greater risk of these things happening now. Instead of a senior parent asking us the same question repeatedly by phone, she could ask the same question again by text or e-mail. The benefit I see with this problem is that we can save the correspondence and show it to them later, to help them become aware of their behavior.

Young at Web

I'm excited about the number of seniors engaging in digital life today. Without seniors, where would we all be? I think the blend of seniors' unique skills as offline community builders, the time they have available to learn new tools, and their eagerness to connect is actually an ideal combination. In fact, I wouldn't be surprised to see more businesses marketing to seniors online in the next few years as the majority of seniors become active online. It is a new world online, but it's one with vast possibilities for all ages and abilities.

No one is too old to go online. On the contrary, more octogenarian-plus users are online than you might think. No one can tell me they're too old to go online because I know it's possible for even the oldest of us to give it a whirl. Like Florence Detlor, who's 103 years old as I write this. She e-mails regularly and is on Facebook. Florence is my brother-in-law's great aunt, and she lives in Menlo Park, California, not far from Facebook headquarters. She began using the site a few years ago, and, when she turned 101, I recall she replied to my message on her Facebook Wall and I thought, *Wow, how amazing is that?* She's

Online Communities for Seniors

Once seniors get more comfortable online, it can actually be quite difficult to pry them offline. Keeping in close contact with friends and family is very important to most seniors, and they can find themselves spending hours each day online sending e-mail, organizing photos, reading news, checking the weather, and playing games. All of the favorite games we grew up with are now online. If you're a fan of solitaire, backgammon, bridge, or checkers, you can play them all online—by yourself or with others. Since most seniors are retired, they tend to spend a lot of time managing their finances and investments. Seniors are also becoming more comfortable at curating and sharing videos online.

Online shopping is one of the best tools for seniors with limited abilities. We'll cover more about that in the next few chapters, but some of the deal sites have become very popular for seniors. Daily deals can come by e-mail, you can subscribe to them on Facebook or other social networks, and you can view them on websites and blogs. Some example sites include Groupon, LivingSocial, ebates, and Juice in the City.

Senior communities are growing online. AARP has a large network. Senior.com is another. Eons, an early social network targeting baby boomers and users over forty, has closed, but they may reopen at some point in the future. Many seniors also find Etsy to be a wonderful site—it's an incredible exchange of people who make, buy, and sell homemade crafts. I'll explain more about online communities in Chapter Eight: Community Is the Key, and online selling will be covered in Chapter Seven: There's No Business Like E-Business. For seniors who want to explore the world of online dating, please refer to Chapter Three: Love in the Time of Messaging. Most sites have age designations, so seniors can be matched with the right age group.

traveled the world and met all kinds of fascinating people, and I've always been impressed by how sharp her mind has been in her nineties and beyond. I knew a couple of friends at Facebook, so I decided to see if I could find out if Florence was possibly the oldest user on the site. I knew they would have information on their users' ages, so it seemed like an easy thing to figure out.

If Florence was the oldest user, I thought maybe Facebook could give her a little certificate or something fun to mark the achievement. If she felt up to it, I thought maybe she could get a tour of Facebook since she lives close by. At Florence's age, I didn't know if she would be interested in any of that, but I asked her niece, and she said it couldn't hurt to try. So I got in touch with my friends at Facebook, who connected us with their communications department. The next thing I knew, Florence was making national headlines in *USA Today* and other U.S. and international publications. One night, my husband called me up while on a business trip and said, "I just saw your picture on *The Tonight Show*." I was tired and confused. "What?" He explained that they had blown up a photo of Florence's Facebook page and there I was, shown as one of her friends. It was an amusing moment, to be sure.

Florence was soon offered a special tour of Facebook, where she had her picture taken with Mark Zuckerberg and Sheryl Sandberg, Facebook's CEO and COO. Ever the adventurer, she had a big smile on her face, and she was very gracious to everyone she met. When asked about what she thinks of social media, Florence once said, "I just want it to be meaningful." We can all learn from Florence.

TIPS AND TAKEAWAYS: The Senior Moment

- Seniors are spending more time online, with half of U.S. adults over sixty-five online and 43 percent using social media.
- Teaching seniors to use digital media is well worth the time.
- Seniors need to understand the importance of basic security practices, like password protection.
- The Internet is great for all ages.

CHAPTER SIX

THE PASSION OF THE WEB

 "Passions are vices or virtues to their highest powers."
—Johann Wolfgang von Goethe, German writer

I've been passionate about technology—particularly information technology, the Internet, and social media—since the first time I ventured online. In my view, a big part of the mystique of this vast digital world lies in the opportunities it provides for exploration of all the other passions in our lives. And it keeps getting bigger. Twenty years ago, I would never have imagined watching movies on a device the size of my hand, viewing fashion shows and figure skating events live from halfway around the world on my laptop computer, or planning travel with a few clicks on the keyboard.

We often think of the Web as a place full of information and ripe with opportunities for entertainment, but it's much more than that. Now we can engage in all kinds of interests, activities, and passions from nearly anywhere. Not too long after Marissa Mayer took the helm at Yahoo! she was on Bloomberg TV speaking about personalization and the future of the Internet. She described how personal preferences will play a greater part in the information you seek and receive. This is one of the reasons companies track what you do online—to curate your experiences on their online properties, sites, and apps. The future of online entertainment, hobbies, and other fun will be largely personalized, personally curated, and managed online. Whether you're seeking news, humor, a good book, entertainment, foodie tips, travel ideas, artistic inspiration, or a new hobby, digital media has it all.

LOL = Lots of Laughs

It's no surprise that one of the first things that comes to mind for most people when they think about the Internet tends to be viral videos—silly videos, stupid human tricks, and, quite often, cat videos. Even people who have never owned computers know about viral cat videos. This has become so mainstream, it's surprising there isn't an Emmy for best digital cat video. People love humor. We crave it—to bring a laugh to an otherwise mundane or frustrating day, to fill the time when we're bored, and to bring joy to others. Laughter brings joy, the partner to our passions.

Ben Huh, CEO of Cheezburger.com, home of LOL Cats and FAIL blog, one of the most well-known global sites for humor, says that people have wanted to laugh "since the dawn of man." (And woman, of course.) "It's the same reason why people tell great stories. It helps reinforce the goodness of humanity." Huh adds that thanks to so much online humor, people have learned better how to make others laugh. "Twenty years ago, you could watch a show and make reference to it. Now we've made media more portable, and that allows people to share, remix, and create something more valuable than the original."

Humor can be found all around us, and, as good comedians know, a big part of humor is timing and delivery, so sometimes just stumbling on a funny article can brighten the day. More purposeful humor, like silly e-card humor (for example, someecards.com), has become popular for women to share online, particularly on networks like Facebook and Pinterest. Humorous quotes can be found easily by searching topics on sites like BrainyQuote. I personally am a big fan of mock accounts, like Twitter feeds for characters from the TV show *The West Wing*, political parody accounts, and other pop culture references. One of my favorites is @DepressedDarth on

Twitter. That account's stream contains social commentary with Star Wars jokes intermixed.

If you haven't ever read *The Onion*, it's well worth checking it out. There have been days I've laughed so hard I've cried—thus the name. One word of caution: If you share stories from satire sites—particularly if you share them on mobile devices—it's easy for other viewers to miss the context or miss that they are coming from a parody account. Some of these satire sites have such well-written articles that you can believe they are just outlandish real life stories when, in fact, they are completely made-up. Make sure to note the source or that it's a joke if you are sharing these types of posts with friends or colleagues.

Mocking technology and online life itself is a common pastime online. A whole site arose called DamnYouAutoCorrect because of all of the irritating and amusing things keyboard autocorrect software can do to what we're attempting to type when messaging others. I nearly busted a gut reading a compilation post on BuzzFeed about "The Thirty Most Hilarious Autocorrect Struggles Ever." A lot of it includes obscene language I'd rather not use here, but some of the software-replaced text is pretty funny. Witness one exchange:

> A: "Are you doing the nutcracker this year?"
> B: "Yep! I'm auctioning kids tomorrow."
> B: "Suctioning kids."
> B: "Birdseed!"
> B: "I'M AUDITIONING KIDS FOR PLAY."
> A: "Wow I am sorry I asked! Hahahahah"

That's why I don't use autocorrect software. I turned it off the first time I got a cell phone and have never ever turned it on in any applications. I'm much more likely to be typing acronyms, technology terms, or proper nouns that get "corrected," i.e., destroyed. I think this software is brilliant in theory and helps a lot of people, like Siri and dictation software does, but, for reasons above, it's just not for me at this point. Still, it can be quite funny!

For News Hounds:
News Readers and Digital Feeds

I remember thinking when I was about sixteen years old that following the news seemed incredibly boring. In retrospect, I think I just didn't like television news reports because they were so formulaic. Once I became acquainted with newspapers, I began to love following the news. Then the Gulf War happened, and I got hooked on cable news from CNN's coverage. When newsreaders like NewsGator, Net News Wire, and feedly came along, I used them to follow news reporting from a variety of sources, including blogs. When social media came onto the scene, at first I didn't use it for news, but, once I followed enough other bloggers on Twitter, it became clear to me that it was going to be the fastest way to receive live news updates. According to one study, 30 percent of Americans now get their news from Facebook. How we ingest information keeps changing.

As digital media evolves, we'll continue to see more opportunities to engage with news, and that provides us with a wide range of options. Most news sites now have ways to sign up for alerts either directly to you—like subscriptions in your e-mail inbox or auto-alerts sent to your mobile phone. Generally, local sources provide the best information, and you can follow their feeds online, even if you can't watch their TV programming or listen to them on the radio (although online radio has been improving in recent years).

You can also go directly to news sources and read articles on their sites, like NBCNews.com and ABCNews.com. Just make sure that when you share news articles and clips, you have first checked the link to make sure it's correct and not a decoy site. You don't want to share the wrong media, and you want to make sure you're getting your news from reliable sources. Hone your "crap detection" skills, as Howard Rheingold, author of *Net Smart*, advises.

The future of digital media is all about integrating different forms of media. It's mind-blowing to think about how social media has changed the landscape of live news and events in today's world, but I think it's a positive change. If you're passionate about news, this is a great time in history to be in this space.

Mooching off MOOCs (and Other E-Learning)

Online education for adults is exploding. Colleges and universities all over the world are building out programs where students can study through their digital networks—either with fully virtual programming or through integrated programs with video chats. MOOCs, Massive Open Online Courses, are online courses aimed at a large audience, built off what was once called "correspondence courses." The ability to learn a variety of topics online has revolutionized learning for many. For example, one Stanford professor's personal finance class was so popular, he decided to turn it into a free MOOC. He received more than 15,000 sign-ups for his class. Sometimes these programs have high dropout rates, so there are groups looking at how to improve online education for adults, but we have to remember these programs are in their infancy and the best is yet to come. Digital education is opening up the doors for everyone, not just kids.

Cuddling Up with a Kindle— E-Books and Digital Literature

I must confess that, although I'm a first-generation digital native, I'm also a book lover, so I'm a late adopter to reading books in digital form. I do believe, however, that e-books represent the future of most forms of literature. I have friends who rave about their Kindles, who love reading e-books, and who can't get enough of their digital book subscription services. Literature is at a crossroads, along with most media. Print publications are nearly all online in various forms now, and it's important to know what your options are because there's so much you can do with the written word online now.

Not only can you purchase e-books for reading on your laptop, tablet, or device (like a Kindle or Nook), but you can also subscribe to services to read books for a monthly fee. Scribd is one such site, described as the "Netflix of e-books." We also have niche e-book subscription sites like Shebooks, sprouting with new opportunities for reading short-form narrative fiction for women and we have sites like

Twitter for
Live News and Events

I highly recommend using Twitter if you like following news, live events, or other active engagement through digital media. If you're new to Twitter and want to check it out, here's a quick primer: a "tweet" is like a text message that can go online either to the public, if your account is set to public, or to a select group of "followers" that you approve, if you select a private account. You can also set up mobile alerts from your favorite Twitter accounts to make sure you don't miss anything they're sharing. I recommend following at least fifty Twitter accounts and committing to logging into Twitter once a day for a month to give it a realistic trial.

In the midst of my research for this book, three major national incidents happened: the Boston Marathon bombings, the massive Oklahoma tornado, and the airplane crash at the San Francisco International Airport (SFO). I was active online—particularly on Twitter, where people share breaking news most rapidly—during each of these events. I cared about what happened in these events, and social media brought me closer to what was happening on the ground. It also provides perspective from real people.

Immediately following the San Francisco plane crash, an active Samsung digital media executive who had been on the plane gave live updates via Path (auto-posted to Twitter) about his experience. Other information gradually trickled in as to what actually had happened on the ground. Most of it was accurate, but some was inaccurate and/or speculation. The downside of digital media being so speedy is definitely the margin of error; reports must be verified. The significant upside is that if you follow reputable news sources and individuals, you can piece together a situation much more quickly and accurately than some of the older forms of news media—especially national television. As I was watching my Twitter stream soon after the plane crash, I saw one person I follow retweet this: "@Luxie313 CNN is talking to people who are sitting eating lunch at SFO, meanwhile Twitter has people who were actually on the plane. #SFOcrash." She made a valid point: now we can get firsthand sources directly without always needing news reporters to be intermediaries.

Planned live events can also be highly engaging. This year's Academy Awards ceremony took full advantage of Twitter, to the point where the host, Ellen DeGeneres, asked a few of the nominated actors to join her in a selfie, aiming to break the record for the most retweeted Twitter post (tweet) ever. After a dozen people crowded together, actor Bradley Cooper snapped the photo and Ellen tweeted the image from her Twitter account, gathering more than 3 million retweets over the course of a few days. They obliterated the previous record, held by Barack Obama. That offline-to-online moment, blended with the online Twitter conversation throughout the event, made the transmedia (the combination of TV and digital media) event a smashing success. In the future, there will be more Twitter-TV integration, showing tweets on TV, and linking videos from Twitter.

Project Gutenberg where anyone can read books with expired copyrights for free. Thanks to these sites and tools, we can now read articles and books of any length on digital devices. I expect the e-book market and online books in general to expand in coming years.

From My Houzz to Yours—Digital Interiors

The digital home used to mean fancy microwaves and thermostats; now it's all about what you can do for your home through digital media. I became completely immersed in the world of digital home design tools when we bought a new house last year. Thanks to Houzz and Pinterest, my pool of home ideas has expanded exponentially from the small selection of home decorating books I had previously collected for inspiration. Houzz is a specialized site and app combination that allows users to create "Ideabooks" full of ideas for the home—whether you live in an apartment, house, loft, trailer, or cottage. You can work on architecture, building new homes, designing for renovations, or just simply interior adjustments like I was seeking. Sites like Houzz are full of images and products to browse that can fill your head full of inspiration for your home. The best part is seeing what other people actually do in real life with their homes vs. just seeing staged interior photos in glossy magazines that defy most people's reality.

I totally became hooked on Pinterest in the past year—mostly because I began using it as a tool for generating design ideas for our new house. I had a blast setting up a "New House Ideas" pinboard with my husband on Pinterest. I set it up to follow other friends and then added more home-decorating boards to follow over time. Now I use Pinterest for pinning a variety of other things I love—including pin boards for digital life, writing inspiration, fashion, and travel—but I've found it most useful for home inspiration and home organizing. With its clean user interface for perusing images, ideas, and blog posts through "pinboards," it's easy to spend hours trolling the site. I like to joke that Pinterest is so addicting, I got a Pinterest injury one night because I was up so late clicking through the site my finger was sore the next day. I pinned ideas for new furniture, art, and more

The Amazon Rainforest—Buying Books Online

For book buying, Amazon isn't the only game in town, even though it was the first and biggest. Now Barnes & Noble has a vast website, and other big stores like Target are selling books online. If you're a fan of independent bookstores and want to support them online, while most don't have the capacity for websites, some have started. Powell's, a famous independent bookstore in Portland, has a website where they sell books online, including used books. Lots of books are available online for free that are in the public domain too. Project Gutenberg is one site where you can download free e-books. Bookshare.org is a great site for print disabled—it provides various forms of accessible books for people who need assistive devices for reading.

As social sharing grows in popularity, social networks like Facebook have added capabilities for sharing favorite books, creating book club groups, and developing pages for favorite authors. Goodreads is a great social network for book lovers—it's built entirely around sharing and reviewing books. Most book reviews are now available online, and you can search for books on Goodreads as well as Amazon, Google book search (books.google.com), and publisher websites. Virtual book clubs are increasing in popularity, as everyone leads busy lives and has varying interests. For example, if you don't have any neighbors who like mystery novels and you want a mystery book group, it's easy to find one online.

through Pinterest and ended up ordering several items for my home from the sites that I had pinned.

On the home-organizing front, I found several great examples for closet organization, kitchen organization, kids' rooms, and garages, and that was a huge help for us while pruning and purging our stuff as we unpacked. We found a phenomenal professional organizer, Amanda Kuzak, to help us out because a Facebook friend of mine recommended her. I followed her Pinterest boards and started reading her blog on home organizing—Kuzakscloset.com. Now I feel like we have a real home thanks in large part to her tips both online and in-person—a great online-to-offline experience. I've also found that most home magazines are now online, so you can go from pinning paper ideas on cork boards to pinning digital images on virtual boards, totally transforming your home in the process.

Fashion Fast-Forward

For years, print magazines and semi-annual fashion shows dictated fashion trends for stores and boutiques. Thanks to the Web, fashion has become much more accessible—and fun—for women and men who like to observe and curate looks. Now, images and video from fashion shows stream online live or within minutes of the shows. Style.com and others post looks from the shows immediately. There are thousands of fashion blogs, online magazines, and fashion-related sites for eye candy and shopping.

"In the pre-Internet days, you really had to live in a big city to experience cutting-edge street style," explains Brooke Moreland, founder and CEO of Fashism.com, an app for crowd sourcing personal shopping experiences. "High fashion glossies were the only window into what was new. There was a disconnect from what was featured in the mags to what real-world people wore. Now, with the advent of personal style blogs, street style sites, and share-your-closet apps, the general public can really have their finger on the pulse."

Polyvore, a popular app, lets you create fashion ensembles or outfits from a variety of options provided on the site. You can share these combinations on other sites, like Pinterest, and you—or your friends—can purchase items in the Polyvore "Creations." Polyvore is not the only site that does this; others allow you to put together outfits from items in your own closet. Some apps have turned fashion into games. There are also numerous sites with fashion tips online. I love spending time on fashion blogs because I never know what I might find.

In 2007, I got together with a few blogger friends from various parts of the San Francisco Bay Area with interests spanning from fashion to art, food, wine, and events. We started an online magazine (fancy word for a high-end blog) called SFBayStyle because we wanted to cover some of the different aspects of eclectic fashion, arts, and culture and focus on what people wear in the Bay Area. It was a hobby project at first, and then opportunities came our way to attend events as media and to place advertisements on our site. It grew to a nice size, particularly since we had a collection of enthusiastic local writers. Our site is still up, although we don't post there very often due to other time commitments, but it has reached more than 400,000 visitors over time. For a style and culture site that began as a group hobby, that's not bad. I encourage anyone with a hobby who wants to start an online publication to do it. You never know where it will lead. (More on blogging in Chapter Eight: Community Is the Key.)

Welcome to Your Personal Gallery: Digital Art

Art connoisseurs may tell us that art needs to be experienced in person, but that can't always be the case. And even a digital copy of a famous print—while not as impressive as the real thing—can still be beautiful. Now thanks to 3D modeling technology, we can even observe sculpture through viewers that allow for rotational viewing. Online galleries have become more prevalent, showcasing art from around the world, allowing anyone to see art from remote corners of the planet. Art information can be found online, along with art auctions, and most art reproductions can be found for sale online.

Artloop, one of the Internet startups I worked for in 2000, developed an online art database and a wireless museum product so people who wanted to learn more about art could go to the site and find out all kinds of information about the artists and their works. Museums could use the wireless product to embed information into onsite walking tours and virtual tours. Artloop folded when the technology bubble burst and funding for new startups ran out, but it was a great idea, and tools like these now exist on other sites and in a variety of museums. Some great resources for buying art online are Etsy, Art.com, Artsy, Artspace.com, and Little Collector. I also read about an ArtsTech Meetup that happens in New York City, where people interested in how social media and technology can expand the reach of the arts get together in person. There's even a hashtag: #ArtsTech.

Fun for Foodies

Foodies love the Internet. You can post about food, share recipes, track food, take beautiful photographs of food, blog about food, find new food, find new restaurants, watch cooking videos, find new books about food . . . you get the picture. There's a whole world of food online. Food blogs, food shopping, food reviews, food logging. The same goes for wine, chocolate—really anything edible or drinkable that people love. It's all findable and loggable or bloggable online.

While we could spend all of our time online learning about food, luckily food is one of those things that you can research in small doses, exploring and marking as you go. Recipe websites alone take up volumes of space on the Web. You can find a lot of great sites on healthy meals, special diets, and anything else that might relate back to food. Meal-planning applications, grocery-shopping applications, calorie counters, the works. Both Safeway.com and netgrocer.com allow you to order groceries online. There are also meal-delivery companies where you can order online. Most of these are local. Blue Apron is a new site working in several markets. With that option, you have to cook the food yourself, but they send all of the ingredients.

Food blogging has become such a huge industry in itself in recent years that there are entire conferences dedicated just to food blogging. BlogHer Food has become quite a popular event, attracting hundreds of bloggers a year. Food bloggers are a dedicated bunch—mostly women—sharing recipes virtually and to the masses instead of just one-on-one with friends on cards. This has allowed for people all over the world to learn about great food from each other. Pioneer Woman is one example. Ree Drummond, who grew up in Oklahoma, studied journalism in California and moved back to Oklahoma to marry a cattle rancher, launching a blog in the process. Since she began, she has attracted millions of readers who follow her blogs about food, parenting, and life in the country. Any kind of food you want to learn about can be found on food blogs.

Foodspotting is a popular app where you can go to a restaurant, review the food, and take a picture of your meal so people can see what they might want to try and whether they want to go to that restaurant. Urbanspoon provides ratings for local restaurants. OpenTable makes reservations online. You can track wines with apps and software, and you can review restaurants through Yelp. Zagat and Google are now partnering to do restaurant reviews. Pinterest has also become a home for recipe sharing thanks to delicious-looking images people share. To get to know one another, bloggers often ask each other what they blog about. My answer: everything but food. However, I do have a pin board called "Yummy Desserts" that has some great dessert ideas.

Beethoven's Ninth MP3—Music for the Masses

I'll never forget the first time I heard a compact disc (CD) recording. My sister sat me down and played The Eagles' "Hotel California" on her turntable, and then she played the same song for me on a CD player. I was blown away by the depth and detail in the sound recording. Sure, there are purists who prefer their records, but, since that day, I've been a complete convert to digital audio recordings. My husband and I are both music lovers, so we've collected a lot over time (all legally purchased/obtained). We're big fans of iTunes for our music, and, as an Apple/Mac family, we've taken advantage of iPods and plug-in sound systems for our iPods so we can take our music with us. For music lovers like us, there's no limit to finding great new artists in digital form.

For playing music online, it's been a bit of a battle for companies to be able to share music, but now that Apple and others have found ways to license music online, you can stream music on sites like Pandora, Rdio, or Spotify, and you can stream radio to your laptop or mobile device. And for anyone who has ever heard a song on the radio that he or she liked and didn't know its name, there's Shazam. You just open the app and hold up your mobile device near wherever the song

In 2013 Beyonce released a surprise album—*complete with video*—entirely through digital media. It became an overnight sensation, selling 80,000 copies in just the first 3 hours.

80,000 copies in 3 hours

is coming from, and it will compute what song it is, tell you the name and the artist. In addition to Apple's iTunes, Google now has Google Play, its system for online music. Microsoft has music you can stream and download as well, and it works with the Xbox.

Toward the end of 2013, Beyoncé released a surprise album—including video—completely through digital media. It became an overnight sensation, reportedly crashing iTunes, selling 80,000 copies in just the first three hours. While this method wouldn't work for most musical artists, it heralded another shift in the music industry. The next few years will bring more intriguing changes as artists struggle with the questions of how to make money off their content and share it with the world. These are not just copyright questions but cultural ones. The Creative Commons allows content creators of any type—writers, musicians, videographers, photographers, etc.—the ability to license content with a variety of sharing features or restrictions, based on personal preference. So if you are a musician and you write a song and put it online, you can make it shareable for free, or, if you're a photographer and you want people to share your images only with attribution, you can specify that.

Most events and ticket sites now provide various ways to purchase tickets to live events or to livestream concerts on digital devices. You no longer have to wait in line at the TKTS box to get discount tickets for concerts and musicals. StubHub and Ticket Liquidator are a couple of examples of sites that sell discounted tickets. Craigslist is another good source for tickets.

Digital Video Revolution

I remember thinking George Lucas was an absolute genius—not just for *Star Wars*, but for naming his digital effects company Industrial Light & Magic because I really felt that's what it was. ILM may have been one of the first companies to bring digital delights to the silver screen, but now we can all do it from our mobile phones. The world of film and video, much like other forms of digital media, is also in the midst of a transition. As networks shift their tactics to suit the consumer audience in different ways, we're seeing series shows like *House of Cards* released exclusively on digital video formats via Netflix. Social media has become a hub for sharing TV experiences—Sundays I find friends tweeting about *Downton Abbey* or *The Bachelor*.

For enjoying film and TV online, there are streaming services on computers and mobile phones, like Hulu and Netflix. Google Play works for that as well and integrates with the Android devices. Apple TV hooks into iTunes and connects to TVs and DVRs (digital video recorders). As I mentioned, Xbox connects to Windows devices. Netflix is another streaming service for movies and TV that can be accessed by subscription. I'll admit it can get complicated to figure out the differences and decide between them, but there are a lot of websites to help with that, and generally it makes the most sense to go with the platform you're already using—unless you're ready to put a lot of time into making a change.

Finding information about TV shows and movies online has never been easier. Most networks and studios now have sites for shows and movies. You can view clips of shows online. There are also sites full of information specific to films, like the Internet Movie Database (IMDB.com). Review sites like Rotten Tomatoes rate films so you can be more informed as to whether you want to go see them, rent them, or pass. And it's so easy to buy movie tickets online now. Fandango saves your information, so you just select the app on your mobile device, find the film you want to see, locate a theater (it's geocoded, so it'll choose the ones closest to you), pick a time, and, boom, you can buy the tickets and go directly to the theater. Just show your credit card, and they'll print you a ticket right there.

The whole culture of award shows—like the Emmys, Golden Globes, Oscars, and Grammys—is changing now too. The entire spectacle is online—live—where you can watch feeds of preshows, live tweet with others, and join group chats and conversations. It's brought award-watching parties to a whole new level. You can now have a virtual Oscar party online while wearing your pajamas and popping popcorn in the comfort of your home.

The Sharing Traveler

I love travel, and this is one area where I've seen a lot of exciting progress online. When I traveled as a student in college, I still used maps and always felt like I didn't know where to go eat, how to say things, or what questions to ask. I carried around heavy guidebooks and maps, fumbling around Europe. The experience of travel has changed so much since then. Last time I went overseas, an average evening went like this: I whipped out my iPhone, checked for local restaurants, put them into my map app, went to the restaurant, used the translation software to figure out the menu and ask questions, used the currency conversion app to figure out prices, logged the experience in Foursquare, posted a photo on Facebook, and had a lovely evening. Travel has become more accessible, more affordable, and more efficient thanks to digital tools.

A Sporting Chance

Last summer when I was on Mackinac Island, an oasis at the north end of Lake Huron, for a family vacation, there was a huge sailboat race, Race to Mackinac, organized by the Chicago Yacht Club. Sailors occupied the whole island as they finished the race. Here's what fascinated me: Before they finished, I got to observe how their families and friends followed the results. Spouses and friends pulled out their iPhones to track the sailors' progress on mobile apps. At the bars, screens projected images of the boats on the lake so we could watch little dots on the map and see results as they came in. I never would have imagined turning a sport like sailing into an online experience, but there it was, offline-to-online-to-offline. Even surfers can now take waterproof cameras mounted to their heads out to sea with them to videotape their surfing endeavors. The world of digital sports is well on its way to outpacing the competition.

For fans of college sports, you often have to subscribe to the college stream for an annual fee (baseball, football, basketball, soccer, hockey, etc.). Other sports have online hubs for viewing, like icenetwork.com for figure skating and tennis.com for tennis. More networks now livestream events for people who want to watch them as they happen, whether it's at two in the morning or four in the afternoon. Prime time isn't what it used to be—now everyone wants to share globally in the event coverage—and, in the social-media age, it's now nearly impossible to be online and not to receive spoiler alerts about your favorite sports. And this year, my dream of watching the Winter Olympics live online finally came true. As a figure skater, I did not take kindly to waiting for every other time zone to find out who won gold before I could see the skaters perform myself. This year, NBC provided apps and online and TV coverage live for multiple events, and it was incredible to be able to participate in the Sochi games from a distance. I was even able to watch from a skating rink in Lake Tahoe.

For general sports news, you can check out most regular news sites' sports sections, like newspapers, or you can go to online sports hubs like The Bleacher Report, ESPN.com, SI.com (Sports Illustrated), and Yahoo Sports. Sports organizations and leagues typically have sites, like NFL, USFSA, and USAGYM, and sports teams have pages, like the San Francisco Giants or the Detroit Red Wings. Many of these sites also include stats from the sports. Everybody's online. Tickets to sporting events can be purchased on venue websites, team websites, and the general ticketing sites I mentioned earlier. And don't forget to sign onto

Travel Planning and Location Logging

Travel planning has become more sophisticated in recent years. Now sites like Expedia, Travelocity, and Kayak have mobile apps. There are so many, I can't possibly name them all. Airlines, like Southwest, have their own apps; hotel chains, like Marriott, have their own proprietary apps. You can plan trips online with these apps, you can use Google Now as a trip-planning assistant, and you can organize it all with TripIt. Then you can log it on Facebook or Foursquare.

It's fun to share where you're going and see what others are doing in real time online when traveling, but it only works if you have mobile devices with you because the location apps are mostly meant to be used when you're on the move. Facebook also has this capability now, which is why some of the previous players in this space closed down, but there's still movement in the space of logging locations and finding friends.

I like using Foursquare especially when I'm traveling because it logs my trip for me—where I went, how long I stayed there, who I was with. It's also good for safety. If something were to happen to me, my husband can check Foursquare and see where I last was. But that's not the primary purpose. The main reasons to use these types of sites are for fun—to log where

your favorite social network during sporting events—everyone's tweeting and sharing and venting together now. No longer are you sitting alone yelling at the TV—you're sitting with millions of others yelling at their TVs, tweeting and venting virtually. It's like one big tailgate party.

Digitally Fit

Living online, it's easy to create a type of disconnect, imagining that the virtual world is somehow not a part of the physical world. We can you've been, to share with your friends, to see friends who are nearby, and sometimes to attach photos to check-ins. Glennia Campbell, expert travel blogger, advises the following:

As a family, my husband, son, and I have visited twenty-six countries and thirty states together, so we are veteran travelers. We used to book our more exotic trips through a travel agent, but now we do everything online, from booking air tickets and hotels to finding a local tour guide or the best pizza in town.

Social media has transformed how we record our travels, with sites like Four-Square and Facebook offering the ability to check in to the most mundane places (I'm at the dry cleaner!) to the exotic (Hi! I'm at the Taj Mahal!), and Instagram capturing every aspect of a trip through a hazy, nostalgic filter. I used to write a travel diary, noting places and people I met on our trips; now, I write a travel blog (The Silent I), with photos that can be easily uploaded into a book through Blurb.com. Instead of a notebook, I carry a phone and note my thoughts real-time through Twitter and Facebook, allowing my friends and family to take the journey with me. I can later create a narrative with these short thoughts using Storify, or write a blog post about my experiences.

converse with people on the other side of the planet, research obscure topics any time of day, play games all night, and visit communities with no relation to where we live. The concept of connecting our health and our bodies to technology and the Internet may seem foreign at first, but it's what a growing number of people are beginning to do, with the physical tracking devices and extensive research tools we have available now. This comes with positives and negatives.

By opening ourselves up to charting workouts online and sharing them with friends, we can create a virtual support group for healthy efforts. By tracking our own health statistics, we can observe progress. By allowing health records to be online, we can see at any time when we had our last vaccinations or what our blood-test results were. The world of health online is just beginning to get interesting, yet there are vast privacy implications to be considered and there is a wide range of misinformation at our fingertips. We're not at the point where the Internet can replace in-person health care, but we are at a junction where we have a plethora of useful tools to augment what we do in our daily lives to support our personal and family health.

Fitness may seem like the ultimate antithesis of life online, but I've found there are a lot of ways to pair offline fitness with online tools to help keep you motivated, informed, and fit. The first and easiest are actual physical measuring devices, like the Fitbit or Nike's FuelBand. These are essentially fancy pedometers that integrate with mobile apps and online software to measure your progress and fitness goals. There are apps with exercises (I'm a big fan of Pilates apps, for example), and the old-school Jane Fonda videos have been long surpassed now by a myriad of online videos on every type of fitness activity imaginable. Pinterest also has health and fitness boards, so you can create inspirational boards with links, articles, posts, pictures, and videos to help inspire you to stay fit.

Game Online

Computers and gaming are like chocolate cake and ice cream. Sure, you can have one without the other and be just fine, but both together can be an excellent combination. Gaming isn't just for teenagers playing shoot-'em-up games or Minecraft until the wee hours, never seeing the light of day. Now online gaming can mean anything from playing Words With Friends (a Scrabble knock-off) on Facebook to exploring an entire virtual world in Second Life. App-based games have taken off the past few years, with everyone from three-year-olds to ninety-three-year-olds playing digital games. Popular games include new favorites, like Plants vs. Zombies, Candy Crush and Angry Birds, and old classics, like solitaire, Monopoly, and checkers.

If you like games online and want to get started exploring, I suggest searching game recommendations on Google Play, iTunes Store, or various websites where they review games. And ask around. See what your friends like. Ask them online, by crowd sourcing or polling friends in e-mail, on Facebook, or wherever you're most comfortable. There are definitely online gaming trends that people follow. While Plants vs. Zombies sounds frightful at first, once I gave it a try—as a recommendation from a trusted friend—I was hooked. After that came Candy Crush. Playing online games has become a bonding experience for my husband, my daughter, and me—we can play near each other and help each other out with tricks for the games, or we can play together (our favorite on the airplane is iPad Monopoly). It's a great way to fill the time and have some family fun.

Digital Delight—A Means or an End?

I suffered a minor concussion a year ago after accidentally backing into a sharp edge on my daughter's bunk bed. It took a week of headaches for me to realize what happened and get it diagnosed. At first, I couldn't deal at all with sounds, bright lights, video, or much in the way of reading detailed articles. I had to scale back my work significantly, but, at the same time, I was bored with resting all the time and I needed some sort of outlet, so I turned to Instagram and Pinterest. They're both essentially filled with pretty pictures. Soon enough, I had developed a hobby of surfing Instagram and Pinterest for fun, liking and pinning purely for enjoyment. I had no agenda, no social media marketing task list, no plan for what to mark. I went where the virtual wind carried me. It was just what I needed.

Now, I generally go on both sites most evenings as my daughter drifts off to sleep. It's a nice way to unwind at the end of the day. I can see what friends have been doing and what things they have been sharing, but I don't have to read any long essays, posts, or thoughts in the process—unless I want to click through pins and see attached articles. YouTube, Vine, Vimeo, video apps, and music apps can also be like this, as can articles or humor, as I noted at the beginning of the chapter. You can spend hours enjoying what you find online without any agenda. We all need amusement and entertainment—flipping channels on TV is one way; surfing the web or social media apps is another. And you never know what you'll find. Here's one tweet I thought was apropos; it's from my friend Raven Brooks, who lives in San Francisco: "Not sure what's more entertaining right now. Twitter or the crazy people on my street yelling things."

TIPS AND TAKEAWAYS: The Passion of the Web

- You can find ways to indulge in almost any passion, hobby, activity, or interest online.
- The Internet is great for all kinds of laughs—not just LOL Cats.
- Give Twitter a try if you want to be more engaged with news and events.
- We've almost gotten to the point where you can find any show, any song, or any video in digital media.
- Now you can design your home, collect art, find new recipes, and enjoy sports online at any time.

THERE'S NO BUSINESS
LIKE E-BUSINESS

 "I like work: It fascinates me. I can sit and look at it for hours."
—Jerome K. Jerome, English writer

I recently heard a story about a woman I'll call Janet. Janet needed minor surgery, so she scheduled the procedure with her doctor and took medical leave from her company. Knowing her recovery would be short, she planned a trip to Mexico after a brief outpatient respite, still citing the excuse of "medical leave." During the trip, she posted several photos on Facebook. Many of her colleagues were Facebook friends, so of course they saw the photos of her lounging on the beach and drinking margaritas. It's not too difficult to imagine what happened next. She returned to work looking healthy and happy. After lunch, her boss asked her to come into his office, where he explained that the company was taking legal action because the transgression involved a government-backed program, not just an internal policy.

Even if Janet hadn't posted the photos online, she might have checked into the resort on Foursquare, or one of her friends might have posted her photos online and they would've gotten out that way. While this serves as an example of how not to integrate your personal and professional lives online, it's really a story about ethical workplace behavior, which feeds back to the theme of authenticity as well as into the concept of brand identity. No company wants to be associated with unethical behavior, and every company wants to be known as a strong, consistent, authentic brand.

Whether you're actively building a professional brand and reputation online, using digital media for business organizing and process management, and/or managing finances online (for personal or business use), you will want to take advantage of the growing number of tools for business and finance use. It's not just about social media and push marketing. You can do a lot with digital partnerships, e-commerce, and financial applications, whether you work for a company, run a small business, or just want to manage home finances. E-business has become an essential component of all business, and, since we all need money to live, the way we manage that money in the digital age can make a big difference long term.

Social Media Is Not (Usually) Your Day Job

We determine much of our professional and financial objectives based on overarching goals and priorities in our lives at the time. I could spend all day reading business-related articles, following my Twitter stream, updating my contact database, making LinkedIn recommendations, and promoting articles on various social networks. While this is all useful to keep me present in my professional world online, it doesn't pay the bills—unless I'm actually building a social media strategy for a company.

Digital media is an amazing vehicle for personal and professional use, but, as I'll illustrate in the final chapter of this book, it can be an incredible vehicle for sucking away all of the time in your day. Therefore any strategy you build around online tools needs to fit within your existing business goals and not add unnecessarily to your workload. Some online systems are well worth the time you spend on them—like contact management and financial management—but others can be incredibly distracting. Take, for example, Twitter. Arguably my favorite social network, I've spent so many hours diverted by Twitter, I don't dare to count them up. The time isn't really spent on

Twitter itself—it's spent following the links, reading articles and viewing images and videos shared. That's where social media sucks you in, and it can be incredibly educational for business purposes, but we all need limits. Set your priorities first, build a solid social media strategy for your business based on those goals, and then act on that strategy, and you'll be much happier and more productive.

Social media strategist and author Tara Hunt describes the Social Engagement Ladder of how people gradually become interested in ideas, concepts, topics, articles, products, people, companies, and brands in the digital world as a series of steps: Aware, Interested, Interacted, Engaged, Evangelized. Just like building buzz offline, this process outlines how we become aware of things and gradually grow to become evangelists for them.

What Happens at Work Stays at Work

According to *The Atlantic*, most workers spend 28 percent of their office time on e-mail. It's gotten to the point that many people can't respond to or even always read all of the e-mail they receive in a day. I receive hundreds of messages a day. Many of the messages are from lists; I've opted to view those messages in digest form because I can't stay on top of the rest of my work otherwise. My husband spends much of his time in meetings, and yet he receives hundreds of e-mail messages every day in order to stay informed about his projects. This can be overwhelming for anyone. I now know a few people who set up out-of-office messages every weekend. In my view, when it gets to the point that people expect immediate responses outside normal business hours, there's a problem. It's not realistic to have those expectations, and it's creating an unsustainable business culture.

I do recommend keeping your business and personal online communications as separate as possible. In some roles, it's crucial, like government jobs with security clearances. In those cases, people undergo training on communications protocols. For everyone else, remember that your employer owns and controls all electronic communications on their networks. So, to keep your personal life private, you should conduct personal communications elsewhere. If you own a small business, then it's not as big an issue. However, you should consider that, if you hire employees, they could end up viewing your business communications. It's easiest if those are kept purely professional. If you ask a work friend to go with you to a concert, do it in a message that's independent of any work topics, for example.

With the proliferation of mobile devices, this separation is becoming more difficult. If you have a business where you are concerned about the confidentiality of information, you must read *Positively Confidential* by Naomi Fine. Naomi is an attorney who covers all of the ins and outs of what employers and employees need to know about confidential corporate information. Beyond that, just use common sense. Be careful about what you text and who you text. Imagine texting that you hate your job to a friend and realizing you just texted that to your boss—you get the idea. Be careful about what you tweet or post on any public profiles. It should always be professional, but this is where the "avoid drunk posting" lesson comes in handy. Overall, be careful how much time you spend on social networks at work. It's best if you can avoid it unless it's a part of your job. Keeping the two separate is important. Or, if you feel like you need to check Facebook during the day, do it from your own personal mobile phone during your lunch break.

Networking Networks— Managing Contacts and Business Interactions

In an age where jobs no longer seem to have the security they once did, it's more important than ever for us to make and keep contacts for cultivating our networks. As anyone in sales or fundraising knows, this is the core of networking. First, I recommend becoming an expert at the e-intro. If you're going to become a top-notch digital connector, you want to be able to introduce people to each other comfortably in a virtual setting. It can be casual or formal—cater it to the audience. Keep it short and sweet. Make sure to cc both

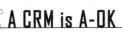# A CRM is A-OK

Customer Relationship Management (or CRM) is a fancy term for a system specifically designed to store contact information. A good CRM can help you with a variety of projects, whether you're working on a school fundraiser or building a large enterprise. It will already have several fields configured that suit personal and professional uses: name, title, company, phone number, address, e-mail address, and so on. A CRM can be basic, like an iPhone address book, or more complex, for managing business relationships.

A great business CRM—such as Salesforce—will allow you to work on team projects and manage team relationships within a company. Many are subscription-based, so you would have to pay by the number of users. It will also include fields for logging when you contacted the person last, what their previous jobs were, what you met about, how you met in the first place, and a number of other configurable fields that help you to do business more effectively.

There are many different online CRMs that can be useful for businesses, including project management functionality. Finding the right system for your organization can take some time; I always recommend finding a user interface that's easily integrated and configurable to your needs while working within your budget.

people, touting good qualities and why they should connect with each other. Digital networking can be a great professional tool. And remember—if it's simple, you're more likely to keep doing it, making it consistent.

When I had a Windows PC, I used a complex contact management system called ACT!. When I transferred to a Mac, I moved all my contacts into the MacOSX Address Book. It wasn't as robust as ACT!, but it was fine for my purposes since I didn't work in sales. Once the iPhone came out, that software synced to my iPhone, and I instantly had all my contacts on my cell phone, so it was worth making the change. Now I use an online service called Batchbook for my business contacts. I also use Plaxo to track contacts online, and it syncs with LinkedIn, another essential tool for tracking business contacts online. (The difference between software like Plaxo and LinkedIn is that Plaxo is more of a contact database, focused on tracking contact information. LinkedIn was designed purposely to be a business social network.) It's all about connecting online and staying informed about what people in your network are doing professionally.

I have become so accustomed to LinkedIn for tracking professional contacts that I can barely remember what my life was like before LinkedIn. Nilofer Merchant, author of *11 Rules for Creating Value in the Social Era*, cites rule number one as "connections create value." A slide in a related slideshow prepared by Tara Hunt reads: "The social era is about connecting people, things, and ideas. It's not how many you reach, it's how many you connect." LinkedIn primarily works to connect people for business purposes. Two new people join LinkedIn every second. What makes that magical is how it brings opportunities to people. Just by posting about what you're doing in your professional life, LinkedIn automatically updates your contacts, which might jog someone's memory about your work and prompt him or her to initiate a conversation about a project or job they need done where you could be a good fit. All you have to do is stay engaged and update your profile. Still, it's important not to put all of your eggs in one basket, so have your own contact management system on your primary computer that gets regularly backed up. As Porter Gale says in the title of her book, "*Your Network Is Your Net Worth.*" Treat it that way.

For Digital Job Seekers

I heard a story recently about an acquaintance whose husband lost his job. In a fit of rage, she blasted the company on her Facebook Wall, saying the CEO was stupid and everyone should quit. Now, you can only imagine how that would look if word got out about her husband during his job search.

Digital Job Search Strategies

If you're looking for a new job, take the following steps before you start reaching out to people for new roles:

1. Update your LinkedIn profile. Make your professional headline something related to the role you would like to have.

2. Check all of your social media accounts for embarrassing photos or posts. It could take a while, but you should remove anything remotely awkward. It might still be archived online, but hopefully you've weeded out the worst-case scenario when potential employers search for you.

3. Conduct a vanity search while signed out of Google (so that the search is conducted as if you were another person). Search your name online, and make sure everything that comes up about you is positive. If you find something negative, figure out the best course for where to address that topic online. Sites like reputation. com can also be of help.

4. Search online for positions that might be a good fit. Get a sense of what you're seeking before you start reaching out to people.

5. Use LinkedIn to determine whether you have connections to people at the companies where there are jobs you seek.

6. Prepare a draft e-mail announcement to your friends about the type of job you're seeking.

Now you're ready to move forward with a more active job search. Send individual messages to friends and colleagues to tell them what you're seeking. Reach out to sites like Monster.com and Craigslist and industry-specific sites like Mediabistro or AngelList.

After she sobered up (one can only assume), and likely after prompted by smart advice from friends, she removed the post from her Wall. Lesson learned. That definitely fit in the category of what *not* to do. Usually it's the former employee who reacts adversely, but it's not impossible for spouses, other family members, or close friends to say inappropriate things as well. Take note and try to stay positive about former employers. Even if you think they were awful, say it privately; never put it online.

Mastering the Virtual Office

I've spent several years working from home and various remote locations. I never set out to work in a virtual office—one of the things that attracted me to Silicon Valley was the energy found in the hallways of tech companies—I liked being a part of that environment. When faced with injuries, I opted to work for myself, and I was lucky to have a computer and the Internet to support me, wherever I needed to be. I've worked from home, in coffee shops, and in co-working offices; they each have unique benefits. Over time, I earned numerous career achievements from my work, and no one ever asked where my office was. The key: Most people don't care where you are as long as you do good work. I know that isn't an option for everyone, but, if you opt to work outside a traditional office environment for whatever reason, make sure to stay active online.

E-mail and social networks can be crucial for working remotely, or in locations apart from colleagues and clients. I end up messaging colleagues on Twitter or Facebook nearly as often as texting. E-mail remains the primary communication vehicle, but it's not the only one. Many of my clients have been on the other side of the continent, or in other countries, so I learned to schedule Skype calls at midnight or send e-mail first thing in the morning so we could keep communicating about projects and not slow each other down. One of my favorite tools, a site called freeconference.com, asks for each conference call participant's time zone in order to coordinate calls properly.

Nice to Skype You—Remote Meetings

A friend recently shared an embarrassing story about what happened during a virtual meeting with his coworker. I'll call him Joe, and he was working from home the other day when he took a scheduled conference call on Skype. Little did he know it was actually a video chat. Unfortunately for Joe, he inadvertently participated in the live chat stark naked. (Lucky for him, the camera only showed him from the waist up.) I share these types of stories not to scare anyone, but to provide some examples where a little common sense and under-standing can go a long way online, particularly when it comes to the intersection of the personal and the professional. Knowing when to separate the two (or use them together) can be one of the most important things you do online.

Skype has become an essential tool for professionals to converse one-on-one, particularly if they're in different countries where convers-ing by phone can be expensive. Google Plus now has hangouts, where you can fit several people in one video conversation online. The newest tool for video chats is an app called Spin, allowing for up to ten people to chat from mobile devices, simultaneously, including sharing photos and videos. Clearly, you need a fast Internet connection to make this work well, but it's amazing how far we've come in such a short time when it comes to real-time video communication. Just make sure you know what you're doing—for example, if you have a phone meeting and you're naked like Joe, make sure the video camera is off.

Winding Up Wikipedia

Wikipedia, the Internet's open source encyclopedia, can be a pow-erful research tool, providing all kinds of useful information. Pow-ered by countless volunteers who painstakingly study the Wikipedia page layout format, standards, and the content they contribute to, it's a real masterpiece of collaborative ingenuity. It's great for filling out kids' grade school reports, looking up tidbits you've forgotten, searching for new concepts, and for learning in general. It is not however, the same as an Encyclopedia Britannica, developed and edited by professionals.

It is a big milestone in the life cycle of one's digital identity to have a Wikipedia page created for you, your product, or your com-pany, so if you're building something big, make sure you're aware of the rules for being cited in Wikipedia. (Your work must be notable, there must be ample citations to back up what you've done, and the person creating the Wikipedia page can't have any official affiliation with you.)

Because the content in Wikipedia is community-driven, it has been crafted by various contributors and edited by others. Journalists, for example, can't depend fully on Wikipedia as a source because not everything in it has been confirmed. College students should be careful not to quote Wikipedia in the event that they look up something that might be incorrect. Businesses should use caution when citing statistics found on Wikipedia.

An incredible idea in theory, Wikipedia has felt some growing pains and still needs a little time to reach full maturity. The last statistic I read showed that only 10 percent of Wikipedia contributors were female. That may not sound unusual in the world of tech, but you have to remember that this is essentially *the* documentation of the Internet.

I created my own unscientific experiment and looked up 30 authors and bloggers who I thought were notable and of a certain caliber—15 male and 15 female. All of the men I researched had Wikipedia pages. Only two of the women did. The other thing I noticed: The men's Wikipedia pages typically included twice the level of detailed information as the women's pages. I view this as a problem. Luckily, the people at Wikipedia are aware of this and they're working on it, but what they need most are more women who are willing to put in the time and effort to learn the Wikipedia system and contribute pages, both about women throughout history and women living now.

If the people you admire, the products you love, or the companies you know aren't represented in Wikipedia, let them know. And if you're so inclined, I encourage you to take a closer look at the guidelines for contributing to Wikipedia. The Web is what we make it.

B2D = Business to Digital

Since this book isn't primarily a business book, I'll keep this part simple. I can't think of any business that would not benefit from some sort of basic online presence these days. It doesn't need to be anything complex, but even my physical therapist, who has an entirely word-of-mouth business, admitted to me recently that she needs a website.

Putting your business online does several things for you:

- It allows people who already know about you to find you easily.
- It validates that your business actually does exist, thereby giving you additional credibility.
- It allows those who want to find a business like yours to identify your business as a potential option for them.
- It gives you the chance to spell out in detail what it is your business provides to others, how it works, when you started, and other relevant information that you might not otherwise want to take the time to explain whenever you meet a new potential customer.
- It allows you to collect information about potential customers and/or clients.
- It gives you an easier platform for providing goods and services.
- It helps connect you with others in your professional network.
- It allows you better access to resources that apply directly to you and that can serve your business needs.

Whatever type of work you do, it's important to think about your needs when it comes to your online presence. Some businesses only use Facebook pages, but I generally recommend websites, or at least sites built on blogs, like WordPress, where you can create Pages with information about your business and Posts with fresh information about what you're doing. You don't need expensive custom designers to make websites or pages look good; you just need to spend a little time selecting a template that works for you. Beyond that, you can decide if you want to get other social media accounts for your business, but I always tell people to start small. Find out where your customers or clients already are online, and go there. Maybe get yourself a simple website, a Facebook page, and a personal LinkedIn profile

Building a Digital
Media Strategy

If you're building a brand or business or raising awareness for an organization or campaign online, you need a digital strategy. Here is the process I recommend when building strategies for organizations:

1. Determine your long-term plan from the 20,000-foot view, including online brand goals, and identify short-term priorities and projects to be addressed.

2. Assemble a team of dedicated people to work on your project, whether you bring in consultants, friends, volunteers, colleagues, or new hires—ideally they should have expertise in your target market or digital space, although that's not always necessary.

3. Build a robust database and e-mail list with as much targeted information as possible (see the CRM section).

4. Prepare a plan for e-mail outreach, as e-mail is still the most dominant form of digital media for outreach, ensuring that your e-mail is fully integrated with the e-mail list, database, and website (or at least that you can easily use them together, like exporting e-mail addresses from Excel into MailChimp, for example).

5. Create a primary digital "home" for your project—most likely a website, blog, Tumblr page, or Facebook page. Configure metrics for that home from the beginning, and determine a plan for how often you will review those metrics.

6. Integrate any necessary e-commerce engine(s) for payment processing, fundraising, or any other financial transactions that are required for your project.

7. Draft initial content, site and blog copy, and specific language describing your project for wherever you will be sharing your content (I highly recommend including blog functionality on websites—this provides the most options for sharing information short and long term).

8. Develop an outreach strategy that includes connecting with bloggers, online influencers, followers, members, subscribers, etc., and that includes online-to-offline outreach (calls, meetings, events) as well as social media correspondence.

9. Organize events—online and offline—engaging digital community, such as Twitter chats, webinars, blogger calls, and launch parties.

10. Determine three to four social networks or communities where you will primarily focus your energies, and build a presence on those communities (for most businesses targeting women, for example, I'd recommend starting with Facebook, Pinterest, and one more where you have an existing network or community). Configure those metrics as well.

11. Craft fresh copy on an ongoing basis, including text, images, audio, and video.

12. Manage your community; listen to people who are now engaged with your project, product, or campaign and communicate with them in an authentic manner.

13. Revise your plan and continue working in each core area, moving forward accordingly as goals, objectives, and tools change over time.

14. Celebrate successes, sharing small victories with your team and involving your community.

to start. Build an e-mail list. Get comfortable using these things first before exploring other avenues.

Here's another reason to engage online: No matter what you're doing in your offline life, you can always keep going online, to some level of engagement. Morra Aarons-Mele, founder of Women Online and The Mission List, puts it this way:

> Participating actively in online community—whether through social media, blogging, or other social platforms—provides women with a way to forge connections and build their online brands on their own terms. As women, most of us will move in and out of the workforce over the course of our lives as we have children and care for our families.
>
> The Internet provides us with a way to stay connected to networks both professional and personal regardless of where we are or what we're doing. Social media and online publishing can help women build a portable, permanent brand. If you take time off to have a baby or opt-out of a typical career-ladder progression, your online presence can still grow and burnish your professional reputation if you put time into cultivating it well.

Customers are discerning—they don't just want to be bombarded with e-mail that's irrelevant to them—but they do want to know if your company is selling new products or providing new services. You have to build your online presence to be authentic to your brand and to you as a person so that it's genuine and fits online; otherwise, it will just be another spam message in somebody's inbox. Online branding and marketing isn't all about pushing your message out to potential customers. In fact, 86 percent of customers want to engage retail brands via mobile and/or social channels.

I could share a lot of stories about what *not* to do online if you're a business, but there are ample examples of that on the Web if you do a quick search. Instead, I'll tell a story of how Beki Hastings of The Rusted Chain Jewelry took her small business online:

We live in the middle of rural Kansas, but I have a very successful jewelry business run only online, thanks to the fact that I started blogging about jewelry in 2006. We now ship worldwide weekly. That would never happen without the Internet! Our marketing has been online as well. I've branched out into social media and connected with other bloggers to promote our product. Magazines and TV shows have taken notice and featured us, but everything starts online for us!

The Web as a Commerce Engine

People occasionally ask me how to make money online, as if you can pick up a computer and push a button and money will start flowing. That's not quite how it works. This misconception is common among wannabe bloggers. We see these success stories in the media about a mom who started blogging about her pies and suddenly she's a millionaire. That's not the real story. The real story is these cases succeed for the same reasons any businesses succeed: They have a plan, they work hard, they keep at it, they build customers, they attract advertising revenue, and, gradually over time, their business starts earning more money.

With that said, if you don't have a specific business entity, earning money online has never been easier. In addition to temp job listings on Craigslist, some temp agencies have websites. TaskRabbit is a great way to make a few bucks doing someone a favor. There are specialized sites for certain types of professionals, like freelance editors and writers. She-writes.com is one great community for women writers that wasn't built just for jobs, but it has opportunities connected, as does mediabistro .com. Clarity is a new mobile app that allows professionals of all stripes to list their skills and provide phone-based paid consulting to clients—it manages the searches and financial aspects of the transactions.

Most people know about selling used goods on eBay, but you can also sell crafts on Etsy and build stores on any of these sites, including Amazon. All of these options now allow you to buy and sell new or used items. Shipping has become easier too, thanks to apps that will compute costs on your mobile device. Mobile commerce is growing at an enormous rate, with more transactions taking place on mobile devices than ever before, since it's so easy to get online from anywhere and buy or sell when you have a free minute. I heard a story about how somebody bought a car through the eBay Mobile app—something you might not expect—just because he researched it online and finally decided to pull the trigger one afternoon when he had a free minute.

Here's one eBay success story from Cindy Sorley of BubbaCan-Dance.com:

> Making the decision to close my brick-and-mortar needlework store that I was tied to 24/7 was tough. As I saw the rent climbing and a toddler who was tearing the place apart, I knew I needed another outlet. I tried selling online. In one month, I was selling more online than I ever did monthly in the shop. Now I sell to the world, from Mauritius to a small village in Alaska that cannot get stitching supplies. I work from home on my schedule and support a family of four. I am in control. I have also become very involved in helping others to learn to sell online through social media. Along this path I have also found life-long friends who I never would have met without a common goal, making a living selling online.

Crowd Funding and Financing Resources

If you're seeking business financing online, it has never been easier. I will provide a disclaimer, however, that there are so many stories out there about people who have raised money online for various types of ventures that it's almost become an urban legend. Everyone thinks he or she can just start a Kickstarter campaign and raise money for a craft boutique or indie film, but, in reality, it's not that easy. If you have an idea and you're willing to put in the time and energy to get it funded, researching online options should be a part of the plan. Just don't expect the Internet to be a money tree.

Kickstarter, RocketHub, and Indiegogo primarily fund projects.

These can be nonprofit projects or for-profit projects, but they must be stated and confirmed accordingly. Crowdfunder is a great option if you want to fund a small business. SoMoLend is a more banklike lending site. Appbackr backs app development exclusively. AngelList allows you to raise seed funds for a high-growth business model. While some entrepreneurs and creative professionals have been highly successful raising funds entirely online, most people who embark on these types of campaigns are successful by combining online and offline fundraising. I do believe that crowd funding and open investment platforms provide for more equal opportunities for women and minorities, and I hope that as the culture shifts to include more virtual funding models, this will bring greater diversity to the startup community.

By the time this book is published, I expect crowd funding to have evolved more fully, thanks to the fact that online financial management software is becoming more sophisticated. I can only assume the digital media shakeup will still be taking place, with advertising shifting to more video content, and content owners being pickier about how they share that content. How we transact online is never boring, that's for sure. As business people and financial managers (at home and at work), we will see more new opportunities for growing our finances and our businesses online as the technology evolves beneath us.

Managing Digital Dollars and Virtual Currency

Whether you're managing money for business use, personal use, or both, the level of digital integration we now have available to us for everything from investing to budgeting continues to amaze me. For money management, services like Manilla will organize your financial information, Pearbudget will help you create a budget, and Mint.com will allow you to track all of your assets and expenses. Most important, there are financial learning sites and apps like Money.com (from *Money* Magazine), CNN Money, and MSN Money. LearnVest is a new app that provides a conduit between professional financial planners and users and helps them to build budgets, manage money, and create investment portfolios.

Online Advertising

I would be remiss if I didn't take a little time to explain how online advertising works. First, there are different types of online ads: text ads, image ads, and video ads. The growth of each type of ad has related directly to the speed of Internet access. In the beginning, text ads and basic "banner ads" or flat images were the only realistic options, when most users were still on dial-up modems for accessing the Web. Now that more people have cable modems, DSL, high-speed cellular connections, and in-home wireless networks, more image and video ads have become prevalent. In the future, as broadband becomes ubiquitous and our cities move to even higher-speed networks like Google Fiber, we will see almost exclusively video advertisements online.

Ads are paid either by impression, by click-through rate, or by time period displayed online. I won't go into all of the acronyms that you might see—there are many—but suffice it to say that advertisers pay websites (blogs, online publications of various types) based on either the number of times the ad is viewed (impressions), the number of times it's clicked through to potentially buy products (click-through rate), or the amount of time it's run on a site (flat monthly rate).

Sometimes, bloggers or other sites will sign on with online ad networks because those networks make it easier for them by connecting with advertisers. The ad networks then take a piece of the click-through

Financial communities, money management groups, online investment clubs, and a myriad of digital financial resources provide all the information we need to get moving with our money online. You should only attempt what is comfortable to you at the time. Read up on some of these things and give them a try. I personally have become a fan of DailyWorth, a network for financial learning for women, LearnVest (noted above), and Bloomberg, where I can study or impression pie, but it's a good relationship for all parties because the advertisers make money and have a constant pool of sites where they can post their ads. The content sites make money and don't have to hustle to find advertisers, and the ad networks make money by making the connections in the middle. Generally websites and blogs have to prove they have a certain amount of "traffic" (regular flow of visitors and/or users) to be invited to sign onto ad networks. Otherwise, they're not a good bet for advertisers. If you only get ten people on your website a day, why would an advertiser want to pay you for that? Ten impressions won't sell a product for them.

If, on the other hand, you are an advertiser, or you want to be an advertiser online, that can be done relatively inexpensively. Say you want more people to visit your online store. You can buy ads on Facebook, Google, or other social networks, and those ads will be placed on the pages of whatever market you target. If you want to select married women over fifty in Iowa, you can be that granular with the audience you target. That's why advertisers love the Internet, and that's why if you build your business online, you may want to consider giving it a try. Small business social media strategists advise budgeting a small amount to experiment with Facebook ads in particular. Even $100 can show you whether a certain type of online ad will work for you.

the markets and business side. Many sites allow you to join and learn for free. Also important, you can monitor your credit report online at sites like CreditKarma.com.

In 1995, while in college, I attended a conference on e-commerce in New York City. I volunteered as a scribe to take notes from the conference, and I recall thinking I was in some alternate universe because all of the speakers were convinced that everyone would be

51%
of U.S. adults participate in
online banking.

buying everything online in the not-too-distant future. As someone studying computer security, I couldn't imagine people trusting their credit card information, bank information, and personal data to the Internet, knowing how insecure much of the technology was. When all of these things came to pass and secure websites became more dominant for e-commerce, I slowly came around to the idea, but I was a very late adopter of online banking. I still didn't want my personal banking information online, but, in many cases, the banks already put it there; you just have to choose whether you wish to access your information that way.

Pew Internet's 2013 report says that 51 percent of U.S. adults participate in online banking, and 32 percent of U.S. mobile phone users do so via mobile apps. Automatic bill payment online, online wire transfers, online banking statements—it's all online. You can now even change your address information online for some banks, although changing important information like that usually requires multiple types of authentication so that the bank knows it's really you making the changes. I don't know what we did for paying taxes before e-filing. That's reduced our tax paperwork load significantly. Now you can even track payments online via the IRS website. And for couples, I think digital banking makes it much easier to track and plan finances. No matter who balances the checkbook, you can both be involved.

Now a word about virtual currency. By now, you may have heard about Bitcoin, a digital method of currency that first came into use in 2009. While controversy and concern about its volatility surrounds this form of digital monetary exchange, I expect this is just the beginning of the debate around virtual currencies. According to *Conversational Bitcoin* by Christopher Carfi, "The Bitcoin ecosystem consists of a network of thousands of computers . . . trading digital assets ('bitcoins') among the network members." It works like currency, it acts like currency, and, according to most definitions, it is currency. Some differences: It eliminates network transaction fees, and it can be divided up into incredibly small fractions of a unit to be exchanged. And it's gone mainstream: You can pay by Bitcoin on Etsy and Overstock.com. Don't worry—the dollar isn't going anywhere— but I expect we'll see some interesting movement in virtual currency in the coming years.

Virtual Is Valuable—Investing Online

When investment firms first went online, the sites were all clunky, full of numbers and what I always felt was off-putting user interfaces, making only the savviest of financial wizards comfortable using the sites. That wasn't exactly the case, but they weren't inviting sites, let's put it that way. Now, that's changing. Sites like Schwab and eTrade have become easier to use. Bloomberg, CNBC online, and Morningstar provide more detailed market information, and anyone who wants to stay on top of markets and investments can do so with minimal effort.

For people who want customized investment management without the high cost of individual financial planners and advisors, enter WealthFront. WealthFront is built off the concept that slow and steady wins the race. As Adam Nash, WealthFront's CEO, puts it, "Most online sites for investing, unfortunately, are selling the idea that 'you can beat the market.' The reality is that beating the market is a fool's errand. Prudent saving and investing regularly into a low-fee, tax-efficient, diversified portfolio is the right long-term strategy. The average investor underperforms the market by over 3 percent over time—a combination of high fees and bad market timing." Nash emphasizes, particularly for new investors, that "they'll be more successful if they *don't* mimic the trading patterns they see online."

The Wild Wired World of Real Estate

Buying a home is one of the biggest—if not *the* biggest—financial decisions many people make in their lifetimes. Shopping for real estate online has never been easier, more efficient, or more fun. I'll admit I'm one of those people who actually likes to go to open houses (in real life) for fun. I like to see what's selling in my area, how much homes are selling for, what people have done to their homes, how houses are unique, and what each neighborhood is like. It's a fun pastime. I find real estate fascinating—the way markets shift, the way location dictates price, and the way people react when they find properties they like. Given that I'm a digital native, it should be no surprise that I took immediately to online real estate tools.

Each home that is listed for sale has a Multiple Listing Service (MLS) number. The first online listings just included basic listing information. Then came websites like Movoto.com where you could actually see photos and listing information of houses and apartments for sale. A few years later, Trulia, a more full-featured site, was born alongside Zillow, a site (and now app) that shows you estimated real estate values plotted on a map. I love these sites. I've spent hours exploring on these sites—I look at local properties, neighborhoods where I grew up, and other cities that I've visited. Now everybody has apps, and it's easy to find real estate for sale in nearly any part of the United States. My current favorite app is Redfin. That's how we found our current home. I also relied heavily on Zillow for relative price information before we made the offer to purchase our home. These sites can be highly useful and informative. You can make favorites lists, watch what sells and for how much, track open houses, find realtors, and learn all kinds of information about neighborhoods, schools, and anything relevant to real estate sales.

Commercial real estate has been a little behind the curve online, but more sites are now evolving for commercial real estate. These sites tend to be more basic and informational, but they still provide most of what you need if you are a commercial real estate investor or developer.

Brand Consistency and the Long View

Whatever you do with your money or business online, keep in mind that much of it reflects back to who you are overall and your reputation as an individual and whatever digital brand you've created for yourself and the projects you work on with others. Remember Janet at the beginning of this chapter, who took the recovery trip to Mexico? Her story might be a lesson in how important it is to represent yourself at your best professionally because everyone else paints a bigger picture of who you are online. Building a solid social media presence on important networks like LinkedIn and Google Plus, creating and maintaining good profiles on your social networks, crafting a great e-mail signature that highlights your current projects, writing a killer online bio, and refining your online résumé are all crucial parts of your online business persona.

Branding expert Maria Ross, author of *Branding Basics for Small Business*, advises people on the importance of brand consistency:

> Whether you are a company brand or a personal brand, you need to be authentic—both online and offline. Nothing is worse than portraying yourself one way online and another way in person. When your brand image does not match reality, it confuses people and they end up seeking what they need elsewhere. These days, personal and professional lines are blurring because of social media, but that doesn't mean you have to hide who you are. It means if your professional brand can tolerate more controversial, edgy tones and that matches with who you really are personally, then by all means post those risqué photos and comments. By the same token, if your professional brand is spunky, sassy, and smart, you don't have to be formal and stiff in online

communities. Be human. But be smart and consistent about it, and that will help people get to know the real you, without hype or overt selling. Sit down and intentionally think through what your professional and personal brand really stands for, and ensure that guides your actions.

You could be the most brilliant person in the world, working on the most incredible project ever concocted, but, if nobody knows about it, it will never see the light of day. Being online isn't all about marketing, so you don't have to always think about it that way, but it is about awareness. You want your network to know what you have done and what you're doing now to boost your opportunities for the future.

TIPS AND TAKEAWAYS:

There's No Business Like E-Business

- When in doubt, keep business and personal digital life separate—separate e-mail and separate time for digital projects.
- Build any social media strategy with your short- and long-term goals in mind.
- Don't be afraid to advertise and raise money online—take it slowly, iterating as needed.
- Manage your digital finances in whatever way fits with your comfort level, interest, and expertise.
- Always assume your business will be seen by others, so keep it positive and authentic with your brand.

COMMUNITY IS THE KEY

 "We live in such a global village that you can find
like-minded people anywhere you go."
—Rachel McAdams, actor

A few years ago, Anne-Marie Fowler, a gifted communications and policy expert who regularly shared her thoughts about important economic topics on Facebook, disappeared from Facebook for almost a week. Friends started posting on her page and sending her notes. They were worried. As it turned out, there was a reason to worry. Fowler had experienced an acute cardiac event, a mitral valve and left-sided heart failure, which almost ended her life. A congenital heart defect perceived to be of little to no consequence was suddenly an enormous danger. She was unconscious and on life support. Her family had gathered and was preparing for bad news. "I pulled through in what I am still told was a miracle," Fowler said. She continued:

> About forty-eight hours after I woke up, I was given my iPhone and laptop back. I logged in, and I was speechless. This is not a normal condition for me. I write speeches for others professionally, within a communications and strategy consulting practice. I was faced with having to describe, from a hospital bed, what it was like to wake up. And know I hadn't died. I was also faced

with more love and letters and inspiring photos than I'd ever expected. My logins to social media were like a first-ever glance into a new and sparkly world. One I'd been in before, but not ever really seen. This was no longer about my opinions and how artfully they were conveyed. It was about something else. This was all so much bigger.

Communities come in many shapes and forms, from small groups to vast collections of like-minded individuals. Many people—even those who are active online—think of communities only in terms of those that they participate in physically, in-person. As a digital native, I think about the concept of community from a different perspective because my early experience online taught me that the best communities come from people with like-minded ideas or goals, not necessarily from geography. I also learned that the very best communities consist of both online and offline components, adjusted to fit your needs.

In Anne-Marie's case, her community was friends and colleagues all over the country, nurturing and encouraging her when she needed them. For others, communities take the form of confidantes, support groups, sounding boards, or just groups with shared interests. An online community might be a group of five people or a network of five million. As long as there are commonalities, you can work together and help each other in a variety of ways.

The Digital Aha Moment

As an awkward fourteen-year-old girl entering high school, I had braces, frizzy red hair, and a lanky frame. I had a few friends from middle school, but, as someone who spent my time either on my computer or figure skating, I was a bit of a social pariah. I wasn't a complete outcast; I just didn't feel like I fit in with the majority of kids. My family had recently upgraded to an Amiga computer, so my parents signed me up with a computer tutor to teach me more advanced programming languages (C and LISP, for those who are curious), and one day, my tutor took me to a local Kansas City Amiga Users Group meeting. That's when the brave new world opened up for me.

Somehow at that meeting, I learned about community BBSes. I could call them with my shiny new 1200 baud modem and post messages. These are best described as a precursor to modern blogs. So I got a few numbers to call from my computer and began conversing with some people on a BBS called The 64th Dimension, a play on the Commodore 64 computer. The Systems Operator (aka owner) or SysOp of the BBS went by the handle/alias of Lazarus Long, a character from the Robert Heinlein books.

Laz, as we called him, was a twenty-one-year-old named Daniel Potter (who now goes by Laz Potter). He was studying Computer Science at a community college and lived approximately forty minutes from my house. Still, it was a local call, so I could chat with Laz if he was online, or I could chat with others on his BBS. Suddenly I had other people to talk with about some of my geekier hobbies like science fiction and programming. But we had other interests in common too—music, movies, philosophy, and global issues.

One day, a couple of months after I'd begun hanging out online at The 64th Dimension, Laz invited me to his BBS Bash, a picnic at a park in Lee's Summit. (This was the event I mentioned earlier in the book where my dad chaperoned me to make sure I was safe.) That one event taught me how to turn my online community into an offline one. Through my BBS friends, many of whom I connected with that day in that park, I had found my first true community—a community that soon extended to making more new friends who attended my high school and who were a part of that same KC BBS group. That day served as a catalyst for my social life—and my life as a whole. I learned that a connection isn't just a phone line and a computer, but where it leads, and who's on the other end. And the best part? Those friends are still some of my closest friends, and we now correspond regularly on Facebook.

That was my aha moment about the online world, as Oprah would say. I got it. I really got it. There have been very few days in my life since that day when I haven't been online conversing with people on some level. Communities can be powerful things, no matter what form they take. The KC BBS community was the first for me, but, since then, there have been many others where I have become deeply involved, built relationships, and gained so much from that engagement.

Finding Your People

We are social creatures. The connectedness of the Internet is what attracts us to it and is what keeps us coming back. In many ways, it is like the fascia in our bodies, surrounding everything, connecting our high-speed society, holding us together. What communities are you engaged in? How do they affect your life offline? How does that translate online? These are good questions to ponder as you think about what's meaningful to you and what communities you might be seeking in your own life.

Twenty years ago when the World Wide Web formed, it was difficult to find much more than static information online. Now we face the opposite problem of too much information, so it's difficult to figure out where to go to find what we're looking for—and often we don't even know exactly what that is. A good place to start is through key words. Let's say I want to find a collaborative writing community where I can discuss writing ideas in a group environment where I feel comfortable. I go into Google in my browser or from my iPhone and start searching for "writing community." A few sites come up: writer-scafe.org, writing.com, thenextbigwriter.com. I check out those sites and they look interesting, but I realize that my women friends have been the most useful in giving me feedback in the past, so, instead, I get more specific with my search and put into the search box, "women writers." That doesn't work either because it just takes me to a bunch of sites about women writers. That's great—very interesting—but not what I wanted. So I try again: "women writers community." I find twenty sites for women writers: Hedgebrook, Wise Women Write, Women Reading Aloud, Judith's Room, Shewrites.

Now I can go onto each of these sites and see which one is the best for me and my needs. Some are more focused on retreats. I don't want a retreat at the moment, but I might in the future, so I book-mark those sites for later and keep moving. I get to the Shewrites entry and see it's the "premier destination for women writers." I like it already. I look at the Shewrites home page, and I'm immediately hooked. But I don't stop there. I take the time to join the site, look around, and I make sure to follow their Facebook page and their Twitter feed so I'll keep in the loop on what they're doing. As a member, I'm on their e-mail list, so they'll remind me of what's going on, and I can keep involved that way. The best online communities today allow you to stay engaged on multiple platforms. So you don't have to just go to their website—you can follow what's happening wherever you may be online. Many of them use Facebook Connect to allow users to join their communities through Facebook, making it a lot easier.

Searching further, I can look at communities in the places where I go online and get a sense of them through the people. If I'm invited to an e-mail group for my daughter's school, I can go onto the YahooGroups or GoogleGroups website where most e-mail lists are hosted and find out who else is on the list. If I'm added to a Facebook group for a nonprofit organization that I support, then Facebook will show me who else in my network is already a member of that group. It can take a considerable amount of time to research communities online, but it's time well spent. Once you find a group of people with the same concern, interest, hobby, or passion you share, it's like coming home. Anastasia Ashman, a digital and cultural content strategist with a deep interest in global communities, has traveled the world and lived in Malaysia. When she came back to the United States, she felt somewhat disconnected. In seeking to reestablish herself in the Bay Area, she told me her unique strategy for reengaging:

> I knew from my previous expat stint in Malaysia that I needed to tap into a local international scene. But I spent months in limbo without local friends, nor being able to share my transition with the people I'd left. This time is different. Now I'm connected to expat-repat friends around the world on the social Web with

whom I can discuss my reentry. I've built Twitter lists of San Francisco people to tap into local activities and lifestyles, in addition to blasts-from-my-Berkeley-past.

Wrapping Yourself into the Right Group(s)

One thing I've learned after thirty years online is that the world of technology is full of buzzwords. *Community* is one of those buzzwords. Some people in the social media business world throw it around like a cuss word, interjecting "community" any time they feel like it, as if somehow that will make a static website more interesting just by virtue of using the word. That's not the case. Communities are all about authentic connection, nurturing, and sharing. In this chapter we'll explore how to find, build, and grow communities for ourselves and those around us.

When my dad died, I soon realized what a strong community of friends I had built. I had many friends who took time out of their incredibly busy schedules to e-mail, call me, take me to lunch, and share their experiences. I'd made most of these friends through blogging—reading and commenting, meeting each other at conferences, and participating on collaborative blogs. We help each other out by e-mail when times are tough. We cheer for each other on Facebook when running marathons. We promote each other's work through Twitter. This is just one community of women I'm privileged to know; because we spend so much of our lives online, we have been more like a neighborhood of women than a virtual hive of people sitting behind computers.

I'd venture to guess that nearly every topic has a community online. To test this theory, I decided to do a Google search for "candy wrapper collectors." Lo and behold, there they were, dozens of relevant links. My favorite is a site called the Candy Wrapper Archive. I completely forgot about all of the candy I ate as a kid and how differently it's packaged now. I took an unintended trip down memory lane, finding old Krakel and Hershey wrappers from when I was a kid. The person who maintains the site has collected, archived, and blogged

Specialized Communities

Most communities stem from some sort of common characteristic or interest. Being a woman immediately qualifies you for thousands of online communities. There are communities for LGBTQ individuals, like gay.com. There are a wide range of parenting communities for parents of all ages of kids, including parenting.com and parents.com, and there are adoptive parents sites like Adoption.net. There are communities for pet owners, and there are religious communities online, like ChosenNet for Jewish people and LDS Linkup for members of The Church of Jesus Christ of Latter-Day Saints. And there are local communities, like those you can create on apps and sites. NextDoor is an excellent resource for neighbors to build virtual communities out of local communities. Even local bars have created online communities. Almost anything can be a community today if you create an online destination where people feel comfortable communicating and sharing about something that users have in common.

about all kinds of candy wrappers. It's one of those things unlikely to be found outside Hershey, Pennsylvania, or Switzerland. While it may be just one website, I also found a Candy Wrapper Collectors Facebook page, several blogs from people who collect candy wrappers, and a few online articles about candy-wrapper collections. Perhaps these aficionados haven't built a bustling online community yet, but it has potential.

The Web as a Gateway

Media expert Cindy Samuels told me she was talking with writer and Grateful Dead lyricist John Perry Barlow once in the mid-'90s when he mentioned that he thought the Internet was "as important as the discovery of fire." Unlike her colleagues, she did *not* think he was nuts. She explains: "For women particularly, the web is the gateway to the tribe—and to change."

Blogging

The first blogs were online logs (web logs, shortened to "blogs") or jour-
nals. Eventually they morphed into short articles. The only real way you
can tell the difference between a blog post and an online article is through
the comment system. These days, blogs, online magazines, online newspapers, websites, and social media sites where you can formulate longer
posts (like Facebook or Google Plus) have all run together. More "traditional" blogs tend to be run on services like TypePad, Moveable Type,
Wordpress, or Tumblr. You can be a personal blogger, with your own blog;
you can be a guest blogger, blogging on someone else's blog, usually as
a one-time thing; on occasion, you can be a collaborative blogger, blogging as one of several regular bloggers on a site; or you can be what's now
called a journoblogger, blogging on more mainstream media sites. I've
done all of these things, and there are aspects of each that I like.

I generally advise starting out as a guest blogger, seeing if you like
blogging, perhaps setting up an account on WordPress, making it private,
and experimenting to see what you enjoy writing about. Then once you're
ready, you can publish the blog, make it public, and see what readers
think. If you don't have time to blog regularly, you can build or join a collaborative blog. If you become a more active blogger or already have a
journalism background, try your hand at journoblogging. There's no one
right path. The important concept to remember is that if you are blogging,
you are creating an online platform for yourself and your writing, you are
building a deeper online presence than just through social networks, and
you will eventually—whether on purpose or tangentially—build a community from blogging.

Blogging really isn't technical at all. Most back ends of blogs now
are much like word-processing software. So publishing a blog post feels
a lot like writing a Word document and hitting "Save," except then your

document gets pushed onto the Internet, packaged in a pretty box that is the design. For blogging, you should understand the difference between static pages and ongoing posts, categories, tags/keywords, and blogrolls. Categories are the overarching topics you're writing about on your blog (or vlog, if you're a video blogger). If I were writing about blogging, I could categorize it in "media" or "tech" if I wanted to go for generic categories. If I write a lot about blogging and social media, maybe my category would be "blogs." You can choose. Keywords and tags are essentially the same thing, but they're terms you want search engines to recognize, as mentioned in the SEO section in Chapter One: .YOU. And a blogroll is just a list of other blogs you recommend.

Other important things to note: Always turn on comment moderation. If you don't, you'll end up with a lot of spam on your blog. Track your stats. See who's visiting. Cross-link, cross-post, cross-promote. Share what you blog on Facebook and anywhere else you live and lurk online. And finally, join up with other bloggers. Build back-channel e-mail groups where you can support each other and share your posts. This is crucial. It does take a village. Blogging is all about community—informing, entertaining, enlightening your readers, bringing them back for more. Blogging is educational, it's empowering, and it's a lot of fun.

No matter what you decide to blog about, please remember the most important rule: Content is king. Plenty of blogs repackage other people's content and sell ads, but, if you want to build a brand, gain readership, cultivate relationships, be taken seriously, attain a positive reputation, or grow a community, you want to focus first and foremost on content. The rest will follow. That, blended with authenticity, is the key to blogging. To learn more, visit my presentation online at Slideshare.net, "First Steps Toward Successful Blogging."

Even simple sharing can represent a community—one photo I shared of a simple path of flowers received twenty-five likes on Instagram, and that made me feel good. It's just one of billions of pretty pictures on the web, but, to me, it was a moment of joy, and my community appreciated that I shared that moment with them.

Strength in Numbers

When I was first confronted with the pelvic neuralgia I mentioned earlier in the book, I was alone in my diagnosis. I had a lot of friends who had other health problems who bonded with me online over the general challenges of living with a chronic pain condition while being a parent and a professional, but I didn't have anyone else I could talk with who had the same exact problem. By the time I had my condition managed, I eventually found a network of support online. It was hugely helpful for me to not feel alone, to have a community.

After blogging about my experience with chronic pain, one day, I received a message from a reader who shared that reading my blog changed her life and possibly saved her life. She hadn't known before that day what was wrong with her. Because her pain and depression—not unlike mine—were so severe, she could not see much beyond living day to day, and she hadn't found any doctors who could help her. When she read my blog, all of the pieces came together for her, and, although I had done nothing to help her physical pain, just having a name for what was probably wrong with her changed her entire perspective, helping her pull herself out of a suicidal state. Never underestimate what a few words and the Internet can do.

One friend of mine shared that her daughter has Ornithine Transcarbamylase Deficiency—a hepatologist informed her of her daughter's condition and told her it was fatal. This mom immediately started searching for everything she could find online. She found two online communities where parents can be informed and patients can interact with each other and feel supported. I know this story is not unique; as patients and caregivers, we all need support, and often—especially when a diagnosis is rare—we go online where we can find others who

share our discomfort and who can help shed light on what we're feeling. As I explain more in later chapters, digital media can make a huge impact on our lives and our health through communities like these, allowing us to make a greater local and global difference in the process.

Alix Mayer and Kim Kooyers met on the Silicon Valley Moms Blog and progressed down an interesting path to create a health-based community. One day, Alix had posted on Facebook that she was buying an infrared sauna. Kim knew that Alix had been struggling with her health, but she didn't know the details. The post caught Kim's eye because she'd just bought a sauna herself, to treat her Lyme disease.

"So I sent her a private message, asking if she had what I had," Kim says. "And the answer was yes. We decided we'd start a similar collaborative lifestyle blog for Lyme and named it SpiroChicks. Spiro for the bacterium that causes Lyme, the spirochete, and Chicks to make it about women and to make it sound fun."

They recruited a dozen authors, and SpiroChicks became a very popular website in the Lyme community. They never thought anyone would think they were "cool," but that's the reputation they've developed in the Lyme community. Since that time, they've socialized together and brought together other SpiroChicks once a month for the past four to five years. They still get together monthly! They just hosted their biggest holiday party yet with the Lyme MDs in the area, the executive directors of the two new Lyme organizations, and other movers and shakers in the local Lyme community.

Gender Bias Is Online Too

There's no easy way to say this, so I'll just get right to it: Sexism is rampant online. In the "real world," you can avoid environments where you know sexism is more widespread, like nightclubs and construction zones . . . (I joke, but you know what I mean). The same is true online, but sometimes, as a woman, it just finds you.

We all have to protect ourselves online, but I find this applies particularly to women. It helps to avoid certain sites, bring our friends along with us to new communities, and learn self-defense strategies to help us along the way. It's nearly impossible to avoid sleazy and rude behavior online, but the right preparation and attitude can take us a long way. It's important to consider how we post photos of ourselves online and how we express ourselves online. As a woman, I consider very seriously where I go at night by myself. The Internet has its back alleys and communities that I would venture to say are unsafe to women. It also has trolls.

Sure, we all get spam in our inboxes, but, if you publish a blog post that expresses any kind of opinion, you can attract a certain kind of publicly rude or defamatory commenter known as the *troll*. Comment trolls are something bloggers deal with on a daily basis that have become both a nuisance and a part of our work—for both men and women. As Godwin's law states that any online argument will inevitably escalate to someone calling the other person a Nazi, I'll posit another unfortunate law of the digital land: If you're female and you post opinions on the Internet, inevitably your posts will attract sexist trolls. There's a certain varietal that is just full of sexist vitriol that isn't worth anyone's time, and those trolls can make your life miserable online. Their goal (or the goal of the people manning the troll bots) is to gain attention and to deter you from what you're trying to say online.

Trolls and spammers latch onto your Twitter account or Instagram and leave rude, offensive comments. The stats show that they attack women more than men. If you write the wrong thing or post the wrong thing, you can inadvertently find yourself the victim of attacks. Even if you don't, a feminine name and/or image can tip them off. It's not just an annoyance; it can result in gender bias and contribute to an overall cultural phenomenon of digital sexism.

We face all kinds of cultural stereotypes and biases in the digital world, as much as we face them offline. The difference often lies in tactics. It's easy to hide in a shroud of anonymity or behind the protective computer screen, miles away from the target of insults. In fact, many abusive trolls aren't even real people—they're bots, or computer programs, designed expressly to spam and harass us. They exist for a variety of reasons, but, inevitably, they can reduce our ability to thrive in our digital communities. In fact, sometimes they target specific communities as a whole, particularly for political agendas.

Ms. Representation, a film about women's depiction in media, helped shine a light on the issue, and the Women's Media Center has done tremendous work involving women and men in raising awareness. Gender bias and sexism online only recently became an issue of attention, even though the women in the communities I engage with all knew of this daily reality. Over the past couple of years, several feature articles have covered gender bias in all forms of media, finally drawing attention to this long-standing problem. Earlier this year, Amanda Hess wrote "Why Women Aren't Welcome on the Internet" for *Pacific Standard*, and several other articles by noted journalists sharing their stories followed.

On Halloween in 2009, I published my own post about the sexist comments I had received on my blog at SFGate.com (*San Francisco Chronicle* online) and why I made the conscious decision to turn off comments following that occasion. In my case, based on SFGate's internal content moderation system, I only had two options: let the comments stay on, allowing all kinds of rude, biased, and derogatory remarks, or turn them off. I chose to turn them off. But at least I had the choice. Being able to control comments helps you fight off the trolls. I have published some presentations on how to avoid comment trolls, but the general rule is always the same: *Don't feed the trolls.*

Don't respond to defamatory comments, ever. The trolls will just keep coming back and getting worse. It's not worth your time, and you must realize it's not about you at all—it's about their game, and you don't want to play it. Put your best face forward and move on. And if this makes you think twice about what you post online in public in the first place, that's okay. Eventually you'll learn what you're comfortable sharing and with whom. If you know how to select who you are sharing with, then you have the control, you make the choices, and you dictate the audience reach.

So why put this in the chapter on community? And why so far into the book? Because community is the key to combating negative feedback on the Internet, and it takes time to build that community. If you venture on a blog for the first time and share an opinion about a topic that someone brings up, chances are you may receive one or two likes, at most, and maybe one follow-up comment in response to your thoughts. If instead you build a community over time through social networks, blogs, e-mail, and other online relationships, you will have at your disposal the help of many more people who will back you up if someone ever attacks you online.

Depending on the type of incident—automated troll irritation or real outright abusive attacks—you can respond differently, by either ignoring the comment, removing the comment, responding directly (this is rare, and is usually only called for if you genuinely made an error), or allowing your community to back you up. Every situation differs based on the parameters of the network, software, users, comment systems, topics, frequency of posts, country of origin, etc., so I can't make a blanket recommendation on how to respond in every single case, but, if you know your community has your back, you'll always feel safer there.

The Wisdom (and Service) of the Crowd

Amanda Enayati, journalist and lawyer, took an unusual tack to respond to an incident when someone broke into her car and stole her bag. Instead of brooding about it and simply calling the insurance company, she took matters into her own hands, searching Craigslist for the stolen items, sending details out in e-mail to her neighbors, and posting information on Facebook and MySpace. She gathered information, and, with the kindness of neighbors and strangers, she was able to collect clues related to the theft. She figured out who had stolen her stuff, and, with the help of the police, they caught the thief. In this case, the thief left tracks both in her neighborhood and online.

In my old neighborhood in Menlo Park, California, we had an e-mail list for all of the women in our book club. Over time, the list began being used for planning the block party, and then it became a neighborhood-watch list for important issues like car break-ins and finding lost pets. We discussed street repair problems and local election topics. And later on, some of the neighbors organized a fun flash mob at the nearby mall with their kids. It doesn't all have to be serious. Community can be fun.

All of this was done by e-mail. It's still the most important tool for online outreach because it goes directly to people. Good old-fashioned e-mail still works best every time. It's about individualized messaging and working back channels—e-mail lists, private messaging on social networks, using trusted intermediaries. You all know this. It's just like phone banking and going door-to-door. Personal connections make all the difference.

A friend of mine lives in Maplewood, New Jersey, where he and his wife are a part of the MaplewoodOnline community. There, people can talk about anything that relates to their community. One day, my friend's wife ran out of gas and was stranded. She went online to that community and asked for help. Someone brought a can of gas to her. These simple stories illustrate how the Internet can bring out the best in people. We hear so much about the worst elements—online stalkers, bullies, trolls, spammers—and so little about these everyday community-sharing examples, when things like this happen all the time. As Brian Solis, a noted digital analyst, says: "Once you become connected, you become part of a connected lifestyle."

Once your community has reached a size where it's building momentum and is approaching some sort of critical mass, you can start to focus on managing, nurturing, and developing that community for the future. Crowdsourcing—either informally for qualitative participation and input or through polls for quantitative data—provides a wealth of information to help you move forward. Then it's a matter of continuing on the path you started. Time creates value. Combined with practice and persistence, as long as the community remains authentic and stays true to its mission, in most cases, it will continue to grow. That growth may not take place in terms of the number of members, particularly if it's a closed group, but it can take place in terms of the relationships that are built and other intangibles that blossom from the community base. Communities of the future are evolving less out of forced connections and more out of commonalities. Since we can now reach millions of people online, it's up to us where we want to go.

TIPS AND TAKEAWAYS:

Community is the Key

- Finding the right community or communities and social networks for you can take time, but it's worth the effort.
- Blogging can open amazing doors to engaging with others on a variety of levels.
- The Internet is not immune to gender bias.
- Don't feed the trolls.
- Lean on your community as they lean on you—that's why they're there.
- Community is the key to a thriving digital life.

THE DIFFERENCE A TWEET MAKES

 "I alone cannot change the world, but I can cast a stone
across the waters to create many ripples."
—Mother Teresa, Albanian-Indian nun and missionary

November 15, 2013, was an extraordinary day in San Francisco. In order to grant the wish of a brave little boy named Miles Scott, the city transformed into Gotham City for a day. Miles, who'd battled leukemia most of his life, had told his mother he wished to be Batman, and the Make-a-Wish Foundation decided to grant his wish. Escorted by Batman, Miles, aka Batkid, saved a "damsel in distress," thwarted a bank robbery, and rescued the San Francisco Giants' mascot, Lou Seal, taking on the Riddler and the Penguin. Miles became a hero to the city, earning a key from Mayor Ed Lee, and President Obama posted his first Vine video message congratulating Miles. "Way to go, Miles! Way to save Gotham!" he said. The production brought tears to the eyes of observers worldwide.

The day of Batkid became a global phenomenon because it combined all of the best efforts of people on the ground and online. City workers closed streets so the Batmobile could clear traffic and follow the Riddler, TV news crews captured video footage from helicopters above, volunteer spectators cheered for Miles in Union Square, the San Francisco Giants webcast the rescue of Lou Seal from Giants Stadium, and the Clever Girls Collective, a local social media agency, worked closely with the Make-a-Wish Greater Bay Area and Twitter to create a digital community around the event.

Stefania Pomponi, founder of the Clever Girls Collective, learned about the event on a local blog called SFist and offered CGC's services to assist the foundation, knowing they likely didn't have the existing support structure for such an endeavor. In the two weeks leading up to the big day, they reached out to Twitter and obtained @SFWish and @PenguinSF accounts to use alongside @SFBatKid to promote the activities. Then they started using the #sfbatkid hashtag. They built two teams of expert social media strategists and tacticians to accompany Miles and to tweet remotely throughout the day. During the total two-week campaign, they tracked nearly two billion Twitter impressions relating to #batkid or #sfbatkid. Batkid ruled the Internet for a day, and his wish not only helped raise awareness for the foundation and for leukemia efforts, but it also brought millions of people together for a day.

We can't all be super heroes, but we can make a big difference online. The ripple effect provides a great metaphor for online outreach because it exemplifies the idea that one person can make a change in her world. The difference can be as small as helping neighbors, examined in Chapter Eight: Community Is the Key, or it can be as big as global political change. The power of the Internet is really just the power of the many, reflected through the ripples as messages travel across the globe through the wires and wireless devices. As I like to say in some of the presentations I give, organizations go online to raise awareness because it's fast, cheap, and easy. There's no other way to reach as many people as quickly and inexpensively as online.

We can all make a difference in the lives of others, and we can reach all the way around the globe in seconds thanks to the Internet, digital media, and mobile technology. How we make a difference is a deeply personal choice, but it might mean volunteering time to charities, advocating for causes, engaging in political activism, writing about important issues, donating funds to projects, sending kind words and prayers to people in need, and individually reaching out to

# Hashtags Explained

Hashtags are a great example of how to become engaged in a specific topic or cause. People use hashtags—the # in front of searchable terms—for all kinds of purposes, but the origin comes from computer programming and old Internet Relay Chat (IRC) messaging systems. Twitter was the first modern social networking site to take advantage of the hashtag, but others have started to follow. You can also search for terms on Twitter and most social networks (Instagram, Facebook, Google Plus, Tumblr), as you can search for tags or categories on blogs. Hashtags are more universally recognized, so if someone's using a hashtag, they are doing it purposely to support a category or meme (an idea of theme propagated online).

A typical tweet or regular category post using a hashtag would go something like this: "A good read: website.com #tech #news." That's the most generic tweet ever, and nobody would likely retweet it, but you get the general idea. Hashtags can be really handy during breaking news experiences or during live events. Sometimes you'll find multiple hashtags used for the same event, like #sfbatkid and #batkid, or #academyawards and #oscars, but, if you follow along long enough, you'll eventually discover the dominant hashtag and can use that.

others. If there's one thing I've learned in all of my years online, it's that one small gesture can make a big difference, and it takes very little time.

Finding Your Place— Causes, Issues, and Campaigns

In your life, there's something that really matters to you. If you care about your family, your friends, your community, there is something that can drive you to become more engaged in making a difference for those people. It might be a parent with cancer, a friend who lost a job, a school that needs assistance, a neighborhood problem that needs addressing, or an issue that takes on larger statewide, national, or international significance. Sometimes these things find us; sometimes we find them.

A few years ago, my friend Pamela Hornik found out her son had what they thought was Crohn's disease (now diagnosed as ulcerative colitis), an inflammatory disease that needs constant attention. The first year, she spent much of her time taking her son to doctors, researching the disease, learning, and advocating for her son and his care. Once he became stable, she became involved in the Crohn's & Colitis Foundation of America (CCFA). She had been a blogger for several years and had an active social media presence, so she used her social network online and offline to help raise awareness and funds for CCFA. Her husband, David, has also shared his involvement with CCFA on social media.

Through Facebook, they connected with others who have children with the same diagnosis. This year, they are doing a run for CCFA on behalf of their son, and they posted a link at Active.com, a site where you can raise funds for active charity events. Pamela also sent out personal e-mail messages to close friends who had helped support CCFA in the past. Through their efforts, she and David have raised several thousands of dollars for the organization, earning them special recognition from CCFA. This is just one example of what you can do when you care deeply about an issue and leverage your existing social network.

One of the beautiful ways we can connect and engage online for things that are important to us is the blending of online and offline organizing, like my friend did for the CCFA. Now with virtual event-management tools, like Evite, Paperless Post, and Eventbrite, we can set up events and send all of the information to people by e-mail. Facebook also lists events now, so you can promote your events there. For nonprofits to actually take money for tickets, they have to attach those invitations to some sort of link where funds can be received for the events, but it's easy enough to do.

Kickstarting Change— E-Petitions and Digital Donations

Before the Web was here, if you had time to give, you had to go to an office or help out by phone, but more organizations are realizing the power of virtual voluntarism and providing opportunities for volunteers to help out causes online. You can help with organization communications, education, and outreach; you can blog about issues you care about; you can share petitions and information through social media; and you can organize and manage virtual events, like Twitter parties to tweet about an issue with others. The more awareness you can build for a cause, the better.

If there's a cause or an issue that you already care about, search for that topic or organization online and find information about how to get involved. To search for reputable organizations for an issue you care about, the best place to start is a site called GreatNonprofits.org. It's essentially a Yelp for nonprofits, where people can review organizations based on their experiences with them. You can learn more about the organizations there and link through to them. The first step to getting involved online is to become informed. Study websites, join e-mail lists, and read blogs. These are great ways to become initially engaged.

Next, I suggest checking out Care2 and Change.org. Care2 is a cause-based site where you can learn more in-depth information about causes and find news and petitions related to those causes. They typically deal with issues and topics of interest to women. If you just want to take action on something you care about immediately, Care2 is the place. Change.org submits petitions to lawmakers, and it's been proven these petitions can make a difference and make change when there is enough action on them. They appeal to a general audience.

Petitions can range from calls to label products to demands for prisoner releases. Anything goes, but numbers do matter. In one case, Vani Hari, founder of blog FoodBabe.com, launched a campaign to remove artificial dyes from family foods. She targeted a petition for Kraft Macaroni & Cheese, working for months on raising awareness

$20,000,000

The Red Cross raised $20 million in 5 days after the Haiti earthquake through text donations, receiving

10,000
texts per second
at the peak.

about the problem. According to Change.org, "After [Hari's] popular petition garnered support from more than 348,000 health advocates, consumers, and concerned families, Kraft announced in October 2012 its plans to remove artificial yellow dyes from at least three of its Macaroni & Cheese products that come in kid-friendly shapes in the United States and Canada." The simpler the request for change and the more active you are in advocating for that change, the more successful you will be.

Meanwhile, if you have the ability and interest to contribute financially to organizations, projects, or individuals that work in areas you think are important, believe me, there are ample opportunities to do so online. Most nonprofits now have links on their websites so you can donate directly. Sites like Indiegogo and Kickstarter allow you to contribute to specific projects, and Kiva is a wonderful site that allows you to support individuals in developing countries through micro-lending. Even if you're not ready to donate right now, it's worth checking out. Kiva makes it easy to start at only $25.

Sometimes you'll just stumble onto something that piques your interest online, and you will opt to contribute that way. One viral campaign raised more than $150,000 for Glen James, a homeless man who found a backpack full of cash belonging to an international student and returned it intact. Someone who heard about the good deed decided to raise funds to help out James, and it became a viral campaign.

Creating a Digital Campaign Hub

Online campaigns can be as simple as a Kickstarter page and an e-mail message sent out by one person to all her friends explaining why she is raising money for an important cause or project; online campaigns can be as complex as what Barack Obama's campaign organization ran in 2008 to get him elected. In reality, most people or groups run scrappy grassroots online campaigns with little to no resources, so I try to advise simpler strategies and tools. If you're building a sophisticated campaign, you can hire experienced consultants who will know how to do the rest.

My basic recommendations include building some sort of central hub, like a blog, website, or Facebook page. In general, I suggest using WordPress to build a basic website that also has blog capabilities. There are a few companies that now offer campaign website packages for various types of organizations, but, before you go that route, I recommend doing your homework. Some of these companies haven't been around long, they don't last, or they're politically aligned in one direction or another (often not transparently), so you have to confirm they fit with your needs. Once you have a site/hub up and running, make sure all of your important content is on the site, and make sure there's a way for interested supporters, volunteers, and donors to get in touch with you so it's a two-way conversation. That's ultimately what it's all about.

One of my blogger friends, a doctor named Enoch Choi, began volunteering on disaster relief missions in 2005 when Hurricane Katrina decimated so much of the New Orleans area. He helped on the ground there and shared much of what was happening through the use of social media, not unlike what CNN's Dr. Sanjay Gupta does on television. Dr. Choi's team helped with the 2007 San Diego wildfires, the 2010 earthquake in Haiti, and most recently with the Japanese tsunami. His online hub is a Facebook page, where he houses information about the foundation he's formed to send groups of medical professionals to help out in disaster areas. His social media savvy has helped raise awareness and funds for those in need in these areas.

Raising Your Voice

If you've ever advocated on behalf of a person or cause you believe in, you know that there comes a time when you decide it's important to become a more vocal advocate. Sometimes that means attending meetings or writing letters; other times, that can mean going online and sharing your thoughts, information, opinions, and stories so that others can also become informed.

Cindy Samuels, content strategist and founder of The Cobblestone Team, explains it this way:

> Women I know have joined together to bring down offensive ad campaigns, change airline breast feeding policies, organize rallies, and support one another in times of terrible loss and pain. I've also seen them raise money in a couple of hours to pay someone's unpaid sick days so they could be with a spouse during brain surgery, and create a community around one remarkable breast cancer crusader that stayed with her and loved her until the day she died, and beyond.

I met my friend Erin Kotecki Vest, who lives in Los Angeles, at the BlogHer conference in 2007. She has more than 20,000 followers on Twitter and goes by Queen of Spain on her blog and Twitter. Erin is a talented blogger, and she was BlogHer's social media and political maven for several years. In 2008, while we were blogging at a political convention in Denver, she fainted and had to go to the hospital. Everyone assumed she suffered from the altitude. It turned out she had Lupus. Since then, Erin's story has taken the shape of a dangerous rollercoaster ride, screaming downhill with surgeries and infusions, turning slightly upward and slowly regaining momentum, before whirling upside-down and jerking back up again. She has taken opioids, antibiotics, steroids, and other heavy-duty medications to battle the disabling disease. Through it all, she courageously continues to share what she's going through with her community online. It's how she stays sane—through photos, Facebook, Twitter, and, of course, her blog.

Even when she's on a morphine drip in the hospital, she's still blogging about her health battles and tweeting her political views about health care because she knows it's important to be heard and she doesn't want to go down without a fight. That's who she is. That's her authentic voice. Authenticity is so important in raising awareness, and Erin is doing an incredible job educating people about Lupus the disease. And she's determined to have the last word. Erin keeps blogging and sharing through social media, as she says, "Not because of an agenda, but because it is my life." She explains further, "I never stopped telling my story. WE must never stop telling our stories, because they MATTER."

Just Say *Please*—Asking Nicely

"Don't forget to say please." That's what we tell our kids. It also works for raising awareness and getting help for causes online. If you're using Twitter, for example, the best thing you can tweet is simply "Please help," followed by what you need and a relevant link. Next most useful: "Please retweet." Simple, effective. It's also important to listen to your supporters, members, audience, constituents, or whatever you call the people who help you and advocate for you.

Children's TLC is a nonprofit organization based in Kansas City that helps children with special needs. They posted a request one day that I thought represented well their purpose and their specific needs. It was also polite and to the point:

> Do you have children's clothes that are outgrown or toys that are no longer played with? We would greatly appreciate your gently used items to share with families at our annual "boutique" next week. You can drop them off Monday or Tuesday before noon. Thanks for all you do to support our programs and families!

Launching New Social Ventures Online

Ten years ago, the Internet was relatively unproven in terms of how campaigns and organizations could reach out. Now, you hear stories about incredible opportunity and growth on a regular basis. Samantha Matalone Cook—executive director of Curiosity Hacked, formerly called Hacker Scouts—founded an organization focused on STEAM (Science, Technology, Engineering, Art, and Math) education for kids. When she first started Hacker Scouts, it was about education because she wanted to provide kids with a real, relevant way to grow and engage in the future that included creativity, innovation, the ability to adapt to technology, and an emphasis on sustainability.

Thanks to the online world, her organization rapidly expanded. She says:

> We made the early decision to be as Open Source as we could so that children everywhere could benefit from our knowledge and activities, whether they were part of an official Hacker Scouts program or not. Word of our org spread rapidly via online press. As a direct result, we have heard from families and educators all over the world. Without the Internet, we would not be able to make the difference we are. It is the catalyst to our vision.

Taking Advantage of Our Networks

Women have traditionally had strong personal networks for making social change. The Junior League is one example. Mary Harriman was nineteen years old in 1901 and was living in New York City when she saw how awful the conditions on the Lower East Side were for immigrants. She decided to do something about it. She reached out to eighty of her friends and got them together to form the first Junior League. Historically, the League (now the Association of Junior Leagues International, AJLI) has been successful at championing issues around women, children, families, education, and health. More than one hundred years later, AJLI has nearly 300 member Leagues in four countries, and these Leagues have made the difference in lives of millions of people while training hundreds of tens of thousands of women leaders. It all began with one woman and her list of eighty friends.

Today, instead of sending handwritten notes by post, we have e-mail, blogs, and Facebook. A few years ago, I served on the non-partisan Junior Leagues of California State Public Affairs Committee (known as SPAC). The thirty-two members of SPAC are scattered throughout the state, so we couldn't meet very often in person. We used traditional offline outreach for advocacy in Sacramento, and my role was to bring SPAC up to speed with new media so we could do all of our internal organizing online as well as some of our outreach to staffers and the media. SPAC worked closely with the Junior League of Los Angeles on a major legislative initiative to create Perinatal Depression Awareness Month in the State of California, and I'm happy to say the bill passed. By increasing awareness of postpartum depression and related illnesses, we can save more lives in our state. By pairing online organizing and offline advocacy, we took a small step for women in the State of California. Now other states are building on this model, expanding outreach for issues important to women and families in Leagues in their states.

What we did with SPAC and California was an outgrowth of traditional advocacy. Most of what you hear about in the media falls under the category of online activism, but the lines can be easily blurred, since activism also engages politicians to make legislative change. It's all part of the amazing new world where we can make what Allyson Kapin and Amy Sample Ward refer to as *Social Change Any Time Everywhere* (the title of their book.) Online activism can take on a variety of forms, from largely decentralized, like the Arab Spring, to highly organized, like MoveOn campaigns. If you have an action you want to achieve, only you can determine what direction to take to start things in motion toward that goal.

You can also build back channel networks. I'm a member of several e-mail groups of women in tech, women entrepreneurs, and women working in social media that have been havens for me to learn and grow personally and professionally. I'm also on co-ed e-mail lists of bloggers, digital strategists, writers, and media experts. The power of these lists lies in their collective social capital, their topical expertise, and a few simple etiquette rules. List names aren't widely shared, whatever is written to the list stays on the list, and everybody must "play nice." Or else the moderator can kick us off the list with one click. Generally, invitations to these lists come through trusted friends or colleagues, so the members are vetted, in a similar way to how you select Facebook friends or book club members. Over time, I've made many friends and allies through these groups, and we support each other's work on projects and campaigns. I call the back channel the secret sauce of digital strategy.

Vote with Your Device—Digital Politics

The first time I decided to volunteer to dedicate my time to helping a campaign, I became totally immersed in how various aspects of the Internet can be used to help with a wide range of causes, issues, and candidate campaigns. I became not only an online advocate but also an advocate of advocating and organizing online. It led me to provide trainings and strategic advice to a wide range of leaders, some of whom ran for office.

Michelle Kraus, digital political innovator, recalls how technology changed her view. She remembers, for example, when Mitch Kapor (founder of Lotus Corporation and cofounder of the Electronic Frontier Foundation) first stood up at a meeting years ago and diagramed silos of data up in the clouds.

"I scribbled as fast as I could to capture his nuggets of brilliance because he was right!" Kraus says. "Yes, we could have distributed computing. Yes, we could have bandwidth. Yes, we could change the world with the power and wonder of technology. The Dreamers saw it, touched it, and changed their lives to be part of the revolution."

Kraus adds that the Internet revolutionized her life by bringing to fruition all of her big dreams of "being able to reach out to an entire planet; making information free for everyone; and changing the way we think with pictures and videos."

Howard Dean first drew attention to the power of digital campaigns due to his online fundraising in the 2004 campaign. Other candidates made strides launching the first blogs and building

Building Solid Online Organizing Teams

Most articles and books tell you about tools, technologies, and techniques for raising funds and awareness online. These are all important things. Often what's overlooked is the people-side of organizing. I've learned from my work with a wide range of causes and campaigns that your team matters—a lot.

Here are a few tips I've put together on building successful online teams for these purposes:

- Put someone in charge of digital strategy who has experience with managing digital campaigns and with managing people, and give him or her a seat at the table with other leadership (policy, communications, whatever the structure of your organization or group may have).

- Build a high-quality team of content creators who can put together all kinds of communications content, whether it be a press release, a speech, a blog post, or an e-mail message.

- If you're building a website, make sure you have designers, developers, and back-end IT expertise represented.

- Recruit a few good online influencers, activists, or organizers who know how to build buzz and have existing networks for doing this.

- Allocate a few diplomatic individuals for replying to comments, e-mail, and administration questions so that you always have someone engaging with people who have inquiries.

- Find people willing to do data entry—you'll need it for building your database, contact management system, e-mail list, and more.

- Take advantage of remote help—there's no reason someone in New Mexico can't help with a campaign in Minnesota if she or he is online—put those people to work on e-mail or data entry.

- Host virtual meetings—use Freeconference.com, Skype, Google Hangouts, or whatever works best for your group to collaborate.

- If any/all of these people are volunteers, treat them like gold, help them through the process, and continually thank them for all that they do.

unprecedented e-mail lists. I worked with one of those. For several years, these technologies were tested by national campaigns before they hit the jackpot with Barack Obama's campaign in 2008, bringing all of the digital tools at the time together and combining them with traditional field strategies to win the presidency.

Now these strategies and tactics have become mainstream, required for candidate and issue campaigns. I generally tell candidates, "You may not win a campaign by being active online, but you can lose by not being active online." In 2008, the scale tipped to where the majority of Americans were doing political research online to determine how to vote. Even local candidates now have Twitter accounts and blogs. Once they become active online, that translates to better digital governance as well.

Kalen Gallagher, who attended one of my trainings on campaigning online, shared his experience with campaigning: "Regarding how the Internet, social media, and mobile technology improved my life—honestly, it IS my life. More tangibly, it allowed me to get elected to office and since then has allowed me to connect to constituents, update them on the work I'm doing, and gather feedback on how I can improve."

I could go into a lot more detail about what successful online outreach campaigns require, but much of that I have already put online in the form of presentations or is beyond the scope of this book, so I'll just note at this point that there are some great resources to learn about online activism and campaigns online, including sites like TechPresident, ePolitics, and New Organizing Institute.

Gov 2.0—Direct Democracy

One morning a couple of years ago, I was checking e-mail and I noticed a message from a White House staffer. She wanted to know if I would like to interview Senior Advisor Valerie Jarrett while she was in San Francisco. She knew of my work for BlogHer as interim political director and as a blogger about a variety of topics. Of course I said yes. I'd heard a lot of good things about Ms. Jarrett from blogger friends of mine who had met her. She's a Senior Advisor to President Obama and the Chair of the White House Council on Women and Girls, so I knew she championed some of the same issues I have worked on over the years. I couldn't wait to meet her.

Two days later, I made it to the Fairmont Hotel for the interview. The moment I met Valerie, I felt instantly at ease, and we ended up talking for nearly a half hour about the economy and jobs, including a topic I care deeply about: workplace flexibility. I felt like we really connected, largely because she was authentic about how she felt about these issues. While the conversation was behind closed doors, she wanted me to blog about it and explain to readers what the concerns were from the White House. They sought to reach more women through BlogHer and to continue a dialogue.

The lesson here is that even the White House needs to engage directly with bloggers, social media influencers, and the general public online. They reached out because BlogHer has built a strong relationship with them over the years and they know the people who work with BlogHer develop relevant content, genuinely listening to what they're saying. They also realize that bloggers have their own opinions on issues and that's okay; it's all a part of the dialogue. Today's government officials understand that direct engagement with bloggers and digital influencers helps them to keep tabs on what people are thinking as well as share their message.

Government agencies and offices are now expected to be online in order to provide services to citizens and residents. I remember the first time I saw the California Department of Motor Vehicles (DMV) website in the 1990s; it was abysmal. Now they have a wonderful system that makes appointments and allows for auto-submission of forms, and it has changed the entire perception of the process of obtaining or renewing driver's licenses in California, something that has never been easy but has in the past been viewed as cumbersome at best. As we saw at the beginning of the U.S. federal government shutdown in 2013, the public became quite frustrated at government websites and social media feeds that were cut off or closed. We the people now expect our government to communicate with us online as a crucial part of our daily lives. This

Metrics, Analytics and Stats—Oh My!

At some point, you may decide to measure the success of your efforts—whether you're running a large scale outreach campaign or managing the digital media for a small organization. That's where web analytics tools come into play. Some measurements are easier to obtain than others; for example, the number of e-mail addresses that have been added to your list since you began—that's an easy one to find. If you've run a survey, your survey responses will provide quantitative, and sometimes qualitative, data. If you raised money, you'll have a dollar amount total over a finite period of time. These are all useful statistics to help you.

I used to abhor collecting data. I didn't like spending my time tracking, calculating, and analyzing information from websites. In the early days of the Web, it was truly tedious work, trudging through arcane logs. Luckily, today's blogs and social networks have more robust, interesting analytics systems built into them, so the metrics are much more fun to explore. I'm now a total stats and analytics convert. Digital analytics can be incredibly useful, helpful, and fascinating.

As Beth Kanter and Katie Delahaye Paine write in their book, *Measuring the Networked Nonprofit*, measuring your actions online can be powerful in many ways:

- It can give you feedback so you know you are headed in the right direction.
- It can teach you what tools and techniques work best.
- It can help you work smarter.
- It can generate excitement for your mission.
- It can help you change the world.

Some of the easiest analytic data to collect are traffic numbers for you and/or your blog. If you don't know how to read these numbers, or if you don't know where to find them, keep digging until you do, or make sure to install a package like Google Analytics. It's time well spent. Once you get inside your data, you can see how many people visited your site, where they came from, what time they visited, how long they stayed, what pages they viewed, and where they went after they left your site. Web analytics are full of quantitative and qualitative information. Blogs are the same way.

Social media stats can be more obvious, as well as more misleading. If you follow one hundred Twitter feeds and only receive fifty new followers, vs. if you follow no new Twitter feeds and receive fifty followers, what does that mean? I recently conducted an experiment with a tweet I posted that happened to receive more than 200 retweets and favorites. I decided it would be interesting to view the statistics, so I used a tool called Tweet-Reach. According to their analytics, that one tweet could have potentially reached more than 500,000 Twitter accounts. I don't know if it actually did, but that kind of data can provide interesting perspective for the use of digital media in campaigns or for business purposes.

When you combine your web stats and social media numbers with other numbers like number of petition signatures, number of volunteer hours, number of e-mail list subscribers, number of virtual volunteer signups, and number of comments received on various posts about your cause, you can create a very detailed picture of the effectiveness of your outreach.

is sometimes referred to as Gov 2.0 (next-generation government), and the transparent part is termed open government.

I have worked on several projects relating to government data online (often called "Big Data" when enormous amounts of information must be stored), opening government information through digital media ("open data"), and educating the public about government initiatives. It all comes from the same concept: engagement. If there is something you expect should be online, ask local, state, or national government to do it. Use digital resources to support local efforts. Work with groups that develop applications based off government data. It can be done.

The premise behind it is that we the people as citizens and taxpayers should be able to obtain and use government data for various purposes. Often it's too expensive for government organizations to build anything of use out of the data they collect or to take on all of the projects they would like to pursue, but, if they just publish the data sets for others, we can do great things with that data. As Nicco Mele, author of *The End of Big* puts it: "Whether it's roads or school improvements (or budget issues), frustrated citizens are mobilizing connective technologies to organize ad hoc projects, sometimes to supplement government activity, but frequently to replace or preempt it."

Many cities and states have taken to organizing data sets already collected by other means and putting them out to the public to create useful software tools. The City of San Francisco published data sets at datasf.org and built projects like SF311.org, then others built on top of that data, creating applications like SFpark that track available parking. It's brilliant and useful. States have developed some unique initiatives as well. The State of Utah won awards for their open government projects online. Federally, the State Department developed a highly sophisticated internal network for all of their employees and embassies to use. The White House initiated the Open Government Directive, and they encouraged people to build applications for a variety of purposes, like Apps for Healthy Kids.

The most important government-related tools online pertain to emergency services. FEMA has ready.gov for what to do in the case of major disasters, all local governments now have emergency information

Keeping Technology in Mind and in Policy

By now, you've heard about the NSA gathering information by secretly capturing data from U.S. Internet traffic, and you may have heard of SOPA, the Stop Online Piracy Act that threatened to change the way the Internet worked, quite likely stifling free speech and innovation in the process. In both of these situations, technology leaders, Internet activists, and technology policy organizations worked together to provide an open dialogue about these concerns and to put a stop to them.

Often these challenges unfold because laws and procedures get proposed by people who don't have technology expertise, and the responsibility falls on the technologists to explain the problems. Some key areas where this has happened in recent years are electronic privacy protection, network security and surveillance, Internet accessibility, intellectual property and fair use, digital free speech and information transparency, innovation protection, and the international-facing aspects of each of these.

No governing body is perfect, so we the people have to participate in the process of educating the policymakers on how their laws can affect our lives. Some individuals and groups—often called "hactivists"—take measures into their own hands, crashing network servers to make a point. Other self-proclaimed "slacktivists" take to Twitter and rant. They're voicing their opinions in their ways, but I don't generally recommend either of those approaches.

I recommend that you take your position as a cybercitizen seriously. These policies don't just affect the big technology companies like Google and Facebook; they can make a difference in who reads your e-mail, how much you're charged for Internet connectivity, when companies can publish photos of your kids, and whether the content you post online belongs to you or to someone else. Technology law and policy will continue to play a bigger role in our lives and our kids' lives in the coming years—stay eductated on policy as it evolves and protect your own privacy and safety with caution.

online, and many agencies and offices have specified information—such as the Department of Homeland Security's cybersecurity hub. The U.S. Geological Survey (USGS) has an abundance of useful information for those of us in California and other earthquake-prone states. The National Hurricane Center has a very informative website. These sites can be extremely helpful, particularly when paired with organizations that support people in the event of emergencies, like the Red Cross. They have a very active online organization and do great work.

Now digital media companies are working with these agencies and organizations to help provide information more quickly. Twitter rolled out Twitter Alerts in fall of 2013, automatically sending alerts to your phone. You can activate alerts from @FEMA on Twitter directly to mobile devices. There are also groups of Crisis Mappers who focus on mapping emergencies, developing technology to help when emergencies happen, and hosting events called Crisis Camps. All of this information, all of these initiatives, and all of this data can be found online. We are all digital citizens, and we can use that citizenship to support public safety and public good.

Now Let's Get Moving

Making a difference online can start with something as simple as a tweet: "Let's plan a beach cleanup this weekend." It can end with a huge campaign to protect the world's oceans and sea life. You never know where that first step will take you. The next generation of digital engagement on issues, causes, or whatever you care about can come from you. Look at how people banded together for Hurricane Sandy. People took to Twitter using the #sandy hashtag and helped deliver supplies, provide support, find lost loved ones, and raise funds for the Red Cross by texting, going to websites, and getting involved.

Here's one thing that politicians like Barack Obama and technologists like Mark Zuckerberg both agree on: They want everyone to be online. We still have a "digital divide" in the United States between those who have internet access and those who do not, and, in order to truly democratize the Web and provide the tools of engagement to everyone, we first need to bring everyone online. Once they are online, they can see all of the ways they can learn, contribute, and make a difference. And it's not just about access; it's about accessibility. Due to continued innovation, we have all kinds of future applications that can help people. A computer-connected 3D printer in Japan now allows blind children to search the Web, helping them feel what they find, like small model shapes of animals or toys.

Every week, I hear a new story about how digital media is helping people. It's not just lip service; online engagement works. If you really want to make change, you just have to get started. Andy Carvin, well-known as @acarvin on Twitter, chronicled the Arab Spring in his riveting book, *Distant Witness.* He sums up the value of digital communities for social change in many ways, but I found this one passage particularly compelling:

> I don't see the Internet as simply a place where stuff gets published or money is made. I don't even see it as a separate place that you enter and exit in and out of the "real" world. It is a living, breathing community of people who don't see a gap between their online lives and their offline ones. And if you connect the dots between the right people, amazing things can happen.

TIPS AND TAKEAWAYS:

The Difference a Tweet Makes

- If you want to make a difference in your community, you can do it online from the comfort of your own home.
- Political candidates, government organizations, and nonprofit causes are all expected to have an online presence now.
- Petitions and digital engagement can raise awareness and get attention from government officials and decision-makers.
- Hashtags can help you keep engaged in issues of importance to you.
- Stay informed—Internet policy issues are also about you.

CHAPTER TEN

WHAT WE LEAVE BEHIND

 "The greatest use of life is to spend it for
something that will outlast it."
—William James, American philosopher and psychologist

In January of 2011, my dad died suddenly of a heart attack. I was totally unprepared emotionally for the grief that ensued. I remember feeling trapped in time—somehow his death didn't seem real to me, yet it was the most real thing I had ever felt— and I needed to make sense of it. In this dreary state, I drifted online; my tendency as a digital native was to share my experience as part of my grieving process. After a pause, I posted the news of the death— making it more real to me, and allowing others who knew him to become informed and to grieve with me. Over time, I shared more details about who he was as a person and why his loss was so significant. As I grieved, I gradually opened up more about my dad's death to the people in his life and mine, which I later shared in a blog post in my column at the *San Francisco Chronicle* online at SFGate.com.

Several readers reached out to me and thanked me for being open and for giving them ideas for how to cope with the loss of their loved ones. I received several notes of gratitude from people whose parents were dying of cancer or who had recently lost family members. The article had personal meaning to them. Their responses touched me deeply. My writing had been published widely up until this point—about the importance of password protection or the latest information technology policy proposal—but this piece touched people on a deeper level. I had an epiphany: I realized that during the many years I had been writing about the impact of information technology on the world, it was my articles about how the Internet affected peoples' daily lives that resonated most with readers. That's when I decided to take a look at all aspects of life online—including how we deal with death—and to gather lessons from my thirty years of experience into this book.

We all face death in different ways, and we all view the ultimate questions of the legacy we want to leave differently. I remember having long conversations with my dad about this concept and what he wanted to leave behind. Collecting memories of his life was also important. In the end, what do we want others to remember about us? I look back at my dad's life and how much he achieved; none of it is written down online. Very little is there about him, because he was an attorney and what he wrote and did was registered more through cases and in the court system before the age of the Internet. Most of what is online about him is information I put there after he died.

My life, on the other hand, is already archived in many ways by what I've written online. My daughter's life will have even more archived in perpetuity, including photos I shared with friends on Facebook and posts I wrote on blogs about her when she was a baby, even though I purposely limited what I've shared about her publicly. The generation after hers will have even more of their lives archived. I read recently about a life-logging camera that takes images automatically every thirty seconds in a person's life. I can't imagine having a camera strapped to my body all the time, like in a reality TV show, but this product will soon be available to anyone.

How do you grieve for loved ones when they're gone? How do you remember those who have passed on? These are questions you must answer for yourself. The meaning of family history, our legacies, and how we grieve online are very personal topics, and, while I can share some examples of how others have done this, ultimately it's in your hands and in the hands of your family and loved ones. Hopefully this chapter will help you to think through the process.

As my friend Jen Lee Reeves at AARP says, "Social media offers the opportunity to leave a digital footprint for your family. When you aren't with us anymore, your digital life is a part of how people will remember you."

Cries for Help

I heard a heartwarming story recently of a man who married his childhood sweetheart. He went through all kinds of ups and downs with her as they grew together, only to lose her to brain cancer last year. He became so utterly despondent that his friends became extremely concerned about him. His post on Facebook about her death produced such an incredible outpouring of warmth and love in the form of kind words and poetry that he says that love shared with him by his friends kept him from killing himself.

Sometimes our friends show their cries for help through social media. When you see the signs—melancholy messages, quotes about suicide, deeply morose comments—don't ignore them. Mentally ill individuals can show their depression or other diseases in a variety of ways online, so don't think that, by ignoring them, you're doing them any favors. Some people just need to vent; others need serious help. If you feel suspicious that someone you know needs help because of what he or she expresses in digital form, it can't hurt to reach out.

Anticipatory Grief

When we know a loved one will die soon, we often find ourselves in a state of what my friend Beth Kanter calls "anticipatory grief." In Beth's case, she knew her father was dying, so she did what many daughters do: She went to be with him and help take care of him in his final days and weeks. She is an online organizer and blogger who speaks all over the world about how to manage outreach, engagement, and campaigns for nonprofit organizations and causes. For her, the grief process began while her dad was still with her. She naturally reached out to her friends online. "Losing a parent—whether suddenly or through a long process—is just horrible," she told me. "I have found my friends—mostly virtual—to be a huge support system."

In many ways, you feel more pressure in an anticipatory situation because you not only have to take care of the person who is still living but you also have to grieve and plan. It can be a huge responsibility and extremely exhausting. Knowing you have a support system is incredibly important. Being able to reach out to friends online—any time of day—when you need them can be crucial to get through those difficult days and weeks, particularly when you don't know what's coming next, or exactly when. Being able to communicate, share what you're going through, and tell stories helps bring you closer to others and helps bring others closer to those who are on their deathbeds.

NPR's Scott Simon graciously covered his mother's dying process from his Twitter account, @nprscottsimon. I read some of his tweets during her final days, thinking how helpful it was that he was sharing such a personal experience. I also thought about how it must have felt to him to have community support during a difficult time. Of course tweeting to that level isn't for everyone, but, in his case, it not only helped him but also helped raise awareness about what it's like to be a caregiver for a dying loved one.

Breaking the News

When someone dies suddenly, it can be very shocking. A few years ago, one of my blogger friends lost her mother suddenly. Her mom had been through a lot—cancer, treatments, remission—and they thought she was doing well. Then in an instant, she was gone. It shocked everyone, especially my friend. She was incredibly sad, but, because she had such a strong virtual support system, she immediately shared the news, allowing her friends to lift her up during the worst months and help her through it. She posted about having bad days and how much she missed her mom, but I could see that sharing her grief online helped her.

When my dad died six months later, I was instantly in shock. The whole day seemed to move in slow motion from that moment forward. Through the fog of emotion, I didn't want to believe it. Logic escaped me, and I was filled entirely with sadness. It began with a phone call from my mom, at an unusual time of day, and I immediately knew something was wrong. Once I received the news, I texted my husband. I couldn't call him because I knew he was in meetings and wouldn't pick up. I don't remember what I texted exactly, but I knew I needed him, so I made it clear that I just got the news that my dad died and I needed him to come home as soon as possible. Even texting those three words, "my dad died," was difficult. My whole body rejected the idea, but I knew I had to do it. From there, the rest of the day I felt this horrible emotional and physical grief, but I made a mental note at some point during the day that I would record what I did and write about it later. I paced around the house nervously for a while, talked on the phone with family members for many hours, and, finally, I had to decide, "How was I going to share the news with others?"

Since we needed to travel for my dad's memorial service, I had to tell people I worked with so they could plan for my absence. Enter e-mail. I might have sent a few private messages on Twitter. It's all a blur now. I passed through the anger stage quickly, and there wasn't anything to bargain for; the only thing I wanted—my dad to be alive—couldn't be bargained for with him already gone. So instead I wrote a long, detailed e-mail message to our immediate family about why I felt lucky to have had extra time with him. Well aware that he was spared twice—in 1953 when he contracted polio, and again in 1983, with post-polio syndrome—I tried to focus on being thankful for the time we had together. Many people wrote me back, thanking me for informing them, sharing their memories of him, trying to soften the pain for me and for them. The personal, one-to-one, and many-to-many written communications helped us all begin the grieving process together.

Pretty soon, a friend sent a condolence note to me publicly via my primary Twitter handle (at the time @sairy, later changed to

@sarahgranger), and I knew it wouldn't be long before someone posted on my Facebook page. So I made the choice—as I do with professional digital media campaigns—to control my message and to post there first myself so that it wouldn't be misconstrued, so that people could have all of the information I had, etc. I posted what I knew as succinctly as possible: He died earlier in the day, it was sudden, and we would be posting more information about the cause and the funeral when we had it. I made sure to post on his Facebook wall so that people would have the information there too. I didn't have his password at the time, so I couldn't post directly from his page.

Some people don't want to share their thoughts online when they're grieving, and that's okay. It's important to know that. But it's also important to know that, in today's social media world, people often post public condolences when they hear this type of news, so it's best to be prepared. The other thing I want you to remember is that grieving online can be done with meaning, and it can be done in a way that is helpful to you and others, not socially isolating. Times are changing. A few years ago, no one shared news of deaths online, beyond obituaries. Now people are beginning to share their emotions online, both in semiprivate spaces like Facebook Walls (Timelines) or on public accounts like Twitter. These decisions are very personal, but know that it's fine, whatever you choose to do.

What happened next still humbles me today. Over the course of two days, I received a few hundred public and private messages on Facebook and Twitter from friends and colleagues as they read what happened. That kindness translated to offline action as well. (Of course it should—I know this from years of working in this field—but this was the first time it had ever been about me. Previously, it was always for a client, a cause, or a campaign.) Friends brought me food and they offered babysitting help, and many just wanted me to know they were there if I needed anyone to talk to. And suddenly, I was a member of a sad new club of people who had lost a parent—people who knew how awful I felt and who didn't expect me to look or act any particular way—they just wanted to comfort me in my grief. To them I owe a debt of gratitude. I couldn't thank everyone individually who wrote on my Wall, but I did what I could and saved all of the messages.

Public Remembrances

My dad didn't have much of an online persona. He retired before the web, and his digital correspondence following retirement was limited to e-mail. But he liked the idea of leaving a virtual legacy behind. He'd explored sites like legacy.com, where obituaries are saved from newspapers (for a price, of course) and felt that something more needed to be shared in digital form when people died. As I was the social media and tech go-to gal in the family, I took it upon myself to grab a domain name and build a basic website for him after he died. It's still a work in progress, and it may be transferred over time, but it's there, including a couple of passages he wrote himself, and I like to think he would have appreciated the effort.

You don't have to wait to create your own legacy or a legacy for your loved ones. You can leave memories behind in various forms, like obituaries, photos, and stories. In my dad's case, he had already written his own obituary and sent a copy to his estate attorney, so all I had to do was fill in a few paragraphs. That made it easier for the rest of the family to focus on planning the memorial service and dealing with their own grief.

My friend Ian Thomson shared a photo of his hand holding his grandmother's hand before she died. He posted it on Instagram, and it auto-posted to Facebook, where I saw it. For me, it was a perfect expression of caring for someone you love, spending time with that person, and sharing what it means to you. I know it must have been hard for Ian to post that photo, but I also know that the experience was meaningful to him, and now he will have that memory saved for the next generation in his family.

The days following my dad's death, I spent a lot of time looking at photos of my dad to feel closer to him after he was gone, but I also felt an urgent need to put together a photo slide show for the memorial service, and, although no one would have thought less of it without the photos, everyone in our family wanted to have something to show, so we began digging through images everywhere we could find them. We bought a high-quality photo scanner and mass-scanned old family photos late into the night in order to build a video that could be presented. The process itself had a healing effect, and everyone who attended the service liked seeing the slide show.

I blogged about grieving online, but I didn't blog about how my dad's death touched me as a person emotionally. That part of the grieving process I only shared with close family members. Every so often, I would post something on Facebook about missing my dad—on Father's Day, on his birthday, and on other holidays—but most of the time, grieving was an internal process for me, shared closely with my sister. We all lose loved ones at some point. It's unavoidable, and it hurts deeply. But we have a choice when these things happen to us. We can wallow in the depths of our worst nightmares, or we can find ways to pull ourselves out. Sometimes it's too difficult to talk about these things, yet a short e-mail message or Facebook post can return immense warmth, and each note of kindness allows us to find a little more acceptance.

We all grieve differently—some more privately than others—and as I was told, there is no right or wrong way to experience grief. It's just something that must be done in order to heal and move forward. While it may seem like a huge leap to share personal tragedies in an online forum, it's almost always worth the risk. There's a reason the word "community" is used so often in the social media world. Now I believe more than ever that those who lean on their online communities for support when they most need it will benefit in the long run.

The Power of Grieving Online

On July 4, 2013, Jeffrey McManus, a noted Silicon Valley executive and entrepreneur, died suddenly. Numerous colleagues and friends of his posted to their blogs, Facebook Timelines, and Twitter accounts with their memories of him, immortalizing him in their words. Many of these memories can still be read online today. One of my friends, Melinda Byerley, shared with me what she went through that week remembering her friend. She explained how different it was from grieving for other friends in the past. She shared her raw experience of grieving online with me, so that I could share it with you:

> I didn't know Jeffrey well at eBay, but we were on Facebook and Twitter early. And we became friends because of social media. Daily interaction, liking each other's posts, debating news articles, and so on. I don't think we would have been friends without it, because we'd have been acquaintances who lost touch when we moved on from our jobs. Since he died, I have been crying with hundreds of people I never met or only knew tangentially.

Then Melinda commented on the speed of everything that happened:

> An obituary was up on Pando Daily within maybe three to four hours of the news appearing on Facebook. An army gathered to do food for the family on gcal [Google Calendar]. A note from Jeffrey's sister appeared on Facebook to let us all know Carole [his wife] was reading and seeing everything we were writing about him.
>
> While I am incredibly sad, I am also really valuing the Internet as a source of companionship right now. It is healing to connect with others and share our grief. I live so far from family that my urban tribe is my family, and he was one of them. The very best. To me, THAT is the story of social media.

A Living Legacy

There are many ways to honor those who die. Often, the loss can be used to raise awareness about causes we believe in, communities we are a part of, and families we know and love. For some people, requesting donations for their church is enough; for others, sending contributions to charities is important. For my dad, it was the Children's TLC, an organization he supported and helped as a donor and volunteer.

Beth Kanter, international guru for using social media for social good and author of *The Networked Nonprofit*, set up a campaign for the Surfrider Foundation in her father's memory when he passed away. She gave it the hashtag #oceanloveearl and asked friends to tweet memories about her father. They had a "virtual paddle out" day, and she created a website at oceanloveearl.wikispaces.com with all of the information. Her father was an obstetrician who loved the ocean, swimming, and surfing.

Sometimes people create communities, blogs, and virtual organizations for those who die—particularly of terrible diseases like cancer. I saw a wonderful online community created as a Facebook group page called "Celebrating Kristi." Kristi was young when she died and had many friends and family who wanted to share their memories of her. Her family participated on the site, but a friend managed the site, and, by having this one special sharing space, it allowed many people to post their thoughts and emotions, feeling comforted by each other.

As you read this chapter, think about what you want to save from your life, your parents' and grandparents' lives, and your children's lives online. Is it more important to have a legacy that you control on hard drives that you backup and save? Is it more important to print photos and store them in envelopes? Would you rather trust an off-site facility where these things are saved for you? Or do you want some sort of combination?

When our kids are infants, we post baby photos on Facebook, we e-mail their first words out to doting grandparents, we take videos of their first steps. These memories can now be captured in perpetuity, and it's wonderful. Now I look back at this deluge of data (because that's really what it is), and, as my daughter ages, I foresee a big challenge of my generation and those to come, as parents, organizing, categorizing, and storing all of these amazing memories in some sort of form that's worthy of future viewing and exploration. My dad held onto old family videos of him as a kid for many

208,000 photos are uploaded to Facebook *every minute.*

years. He had them digitized and spent a significant amount of time organizing them so he would always have those memories. He spent hours, days working on this. And he only had a couple dozen short videos. I have hundreds of videos of my daughter and tens of thousands of photos we've taken of her since the first moments she was born. And it's not just my daughter. I have a ton of images of my cats. What do we do with all of this?

More social networks and websites are becoming savvy to the fact that they must do something with your data when you're gone. Google and others are creating settings so you can allow another person to have access to your account in order to close it or obtain data logs or other important information. Some specialized apps have been developed to be a trove of "digital assets," like Entrustet, a service that will store information about all kinds of accounts so they can be dealt with appropriately after you—or your loved one—is gone. More sites appear every six months. I read a great tweet one day from Amanda Blain (@amandablain): "When I die, I want my tombstone to have free WiFi, that way people will visit more often." She may be on to something.

Pretty much anything with the word "legacy" in it relates back to this topic: legacy.com, legacylocker.com, legacyarchives.com, legacystories.org, and more. What I will say is that, since there's no one standard leader in this space, do your homework, check out a variety of options, and consider backup strategies as well when you undergo

Curating Our Legacies

It's time to consider what type of storage and backup solutions work best for you. While family archival software exists, that's not necessarily the same as curating and saving your individual files yourself for posterity. I try to live by rules I learned as a network administrator. I employ a system of regular backups for all devices and computers, on-site and off-site (meaning, for my personal life, at home, and away from home). At home can include burning CD backups or saving files on an external hard drive. Off-site can mean storing an extra drive with another family member or using cloud storage (saving copies of your data on data storage devices, generally in giant warehouselike facilities), depending on your personal preferences and how often you make backups.

On the topic of types of media to save, historically, paper has been the most reliable way to store things. With the advent of digital media technologies, storage formats keep changing. There are some formats that are more universal for saving digital files, but most files we have on our computers today would have to be converted into those formats, thus the need for professional backup systems. Even if I saved all the important documents in my family for my daughter in exactly the file formats that would be most readable long term, it's likely she would need some assistance converting them back to whatever format ends up being used as the standard fifty years from now.

Lois Kauffman, a professional certified archivist, advises, "Digital files are a garden that must be tended. To keep digital files readable, they must be updated to new software and hardware. Updating digital files requires attention and discipline."

Here are Lois's top tips for preserving important documents and images:

- Paper and pencil are the most lasting medium. Make paper copies of your most important documents and digital images, using acid-free paper.
- Store paper documents and photo prints in a dry, temperature-stable location—avoid basements and attics.
- Black-and-white prints will last. All color images deteriorate with time. For best color retention, use archival photo paper when making prints.
- Build a living/growing curated collection. This is the pool you will draw upon as the years go by, selecting your most precious and favorite photos.
- Name and date your documents and photos in a consistent manner, identifying people, places, and events.
- Save copies of the select photos in folders.
- Name digital files with key words, names, and dates to make them searchable.
- Be systematic. Use a simple folder plan to organize your files.

any kind of online legacy planning. After all, if you want a lasting legacy, you want it to begin with getting the information you want online when you want it, on your terms. Eric Schmidt and Jared Cohen articulate this well in their book, *The New Digital Age*. "In many ways, our virtual identities will come to supersede all others, as the trails they leave remain engraved online in perpetuity."

Diving for Digital Memories

While we're healthy and able to organize our own memories and those of other family members, it's good to allocate time and energy to identify what we want to save and store for future generations. This might mean scanning and annotating old family photos, it might mean trolling genealogy websites to save information related to our ancestors, or it could just mean saving meaningful e-mail messages from our parents.

There are three primary reasons we want to hold onto personal documents and images in perpetuity:

- They're necessary: Important documents like financial and legal information.
- They're historical: Family memorabilia and information from past and present generations that can be passed on to the next generation and beyond, such as family portraits, important honors, and letters written by grandparents.
- They're sentimental: Personally meaningful, memorable, or otherwise emotionally important items, like baby pictures, wedding invitations, and letters from friends.

If there's a disaster and you can only take a few items from your house before evacuating, what will you take? This is not a new question. I implore you to consider it a different way. If you had to save memories of your life in a time capsule, what would they be? Letters, messages, photos, videos, and perhaps audio recordings top most lists. That's what the Internet is, in its way. There's no guarantee that what we put online will stay there, but a lot of sites and services archive data for the long term. That could mean ten years, fifty years, or more, but it depends on who runs the sites and what their plans for keeping that data online are. You can assume most sites like Google and Facebook will be around for the next fifty years plus, but what about after that?

Our generation thinks less about resource allocation than previous ones because data storage is virtual. I look at how my mom takes photos on her new iPhone—she is still very judicious about selecting which images she wants to keep because she came from an era of film rolls and slide projectors. Now we have cloud storage and hard drives with multiple terabytes of data storage capacity, but we have a big problem of parsing and access. The buzz term du jour for this is "Big Data." For a while, all of the technology talk was about storage in "the cloud," and now it's about mass quantities of data. Companies, governments, and now families have to face this giant problem of how to store, access, and organize our precious and personally important data.

Transitions and Ghost Accounts

Every death is a life transition, and, with every life transition, we must reach a point of acceptance and closure. In the case of how you deal with death online, first there's crucial organizing to face, such as closing accounts that belonged to people who died. Sometimes the companies that host the accounts do this. For example, when I was researching Jerry McManus to write this chapter, I noticed his LinkedIn profile had been removed. That was likely done by LinkedIn, but Jerry's wife could also have done it. His website and blog remain.

Many people's social media accounts continue on after they die, until someone deletes the account. One friend of mine called these accounts "ghosts." Think about that carefully. Think about whether you want your online legacy to be ghost social media accounts or something different, and make sure your wishes are included with any final requests. As author Nathan Bransford writes: "Humanity will never be permanent, at least on a cosmic timeline, but as long as our computer servers persist, none of us will truly be forgotten."

TIPS AND TAKEAWAYS: What We Leave Behind

- Take advantage of digital media to leave a legacy for your family.
- Don't be afraid to lean on your online community for support in times of grief.
- Sharing public remembrances can make a big impact.
- Curate your own legacy, keeping digital documents and images in mind.

CHAPTER ELEVEN

A STITCH IN DIGITAL TIME

 "Let's go invent tomorrow rather than worrying about
what happened yesterday."
—Steve Jobs, American entrepreneur and inventor

Nearly every day, someone tells me how over-whelmed she feels by the vast amount of information coming to her online, via e-mail, social media, mobile alerts, and text messages. Sociologists and psychologists now analyze the dangers of too much time online. Not only is this a time-management issue, but it also affects our overall health. And the answers to the ongoing questions about how to achieve some sort of balance in approaching the glut of information streaming toward us can vary depending on the person and how we use all of these tools now at our disposal. Now the challenge of our age is: How do you balance all of these online demands and still create the life online that you want—and need?

According to data from SINTEF, a Scandinavian research agency, "90 percent of all the data in the world has been generated over the last two years." In other words, we have such a vast treasure trove of information at our fingertips now that we could never possibly consume even a small fraction of it. IBM researchers have concluded that thanks to smartphones, tablets, social media sites, e-mail, and other forms of digital communications, "the world creates 2.5 quintillion bytes of new data daily." Your contribution to that data will fluctuate, but, in general,

53 percent of U.S. adult women use social media at least once a week. We're spending less time reading magazines and newspapers, less time watching TV, and more time online. For some women, we're spending a lot more time online. Now that I have shared with you many of the most popular ways you can spend your time online, let's take a closer look at how to best use that time effectively and avoid becoming sidetracked, depressed, overwhelmed, or addicted.

Our time is finite; the Internet is infinite. We can never win a battle over time if we go to war with the Web. Instead, we all have to resort to diplomacy and good judgment. Yeah, that sounds easier than it actually is. On any given day, I wake up to Twitter alerts. I read them before getting my daughter ready for school. I'm then bombarded by e-mail as I try to get settled into my workday. Inevitably, as soon as I'm finally focused and in the flow, zone, or whatever you want to call my productive state, somebody starts texting me. I finally get back on course several minutes later. I take a break for lunch, check Facebook, get sidetracked there, maybe tangentially sidetracked on Instagram. I get back to work, more Twitter alerts. That's my reality. I created this reality. I have the power to decide if or when it's too much. My time is finite. Your time is finite.

If You're Overstimulated and Overloaded, You're Not Alone

For almost everyone I know who has complained of info-glut, social-media overload, data deluge, or any other form of overstimulation or overload from digital technologies, something tipped the scale. It happens easily enough. One week, you're on top of your e-mail. The next week, you're buried under a mountain of 35,000 messages. Maybe you took a vacation, perhaps a work project kicked into high gear, maybe a family member got sick and you didn't check messages for a few days. Whatever happened, you crossed the point where you were previously comfortable managing your information flow. Now you feel stuck.

The average person today is exposed to more information in one day than someone was exposed to in an entire lifetime in the 1500s.

 of all the data in the world has been generated *over the last* TWO YEARS.

This point might be different for everyone. If you live in a small town and one hundred cars come for a car show, you probably consider that a lot of traffic. If you live in a big city and one thousand cars are stuck in gridlock, perhaps that's your definition of traffic. We all have unique levels of tolerance. (It's best not to mock someone else if they complain about "all of their e-mail" and it's 50 messages to your 5000.) According to a stat from the Digital Life Design (DLD) 2013 conference, "The average person today is exposed to more info in a day than someone was exposed to in an entire lifetime in the 1500s." Just think for a minute about what that means for our brains alone.

Xeni Jardin, founding partner and coeditor at the popular collaborative blog Boing Boing, posted on Twitter recently: "At dinner, a friend couldn't remember the name of someone we'd met once; Instagram became a memory bank. Scroll, find snapshot, tagged names." Enter the Web, our backup brains. I think this is a great example of how all of the extra information, data, and images we collect, curate, and log online can be put to use. The deluge of information is only as overwhelming as we let it become. I'll let the neurologists, psychiatrists, sociologists, and other researchers debate what all of this information is doing to our brains and the way we think and act. For now, I say use it to your advantage.

When You Hide Behind Your iPhone

I'll admit I have used my iPhone to avoid being social in person some-times. This is really common behavior in Silicon Valley, and I'm seeing it become more prevalent elsewhere. I'm an introvert, and a lot of the people who work in the tech field are introverts, so it's understandable how we've shifted to these behaviors. It's also easy to use mobile and social tech to quell boredom. If I'm sitting at a café waiting for a friend, why wouldn't I go to my handy dandy device to check messages or surf websites?

Some people might appear to be social media addicts because they spend so much time online, when really it's become a habit of escap-ism and/or boredom. You don't want to work, you're waiting for the train, you're uncomfortable at a party? Check Facebook, e-mail, etc. . . . While it is becoming more socially acceptable to do this in some cir-cumstances, like on commuter trains, it can also be dangerous. In late September of last year, a man was shot on a Muni train in San Francisco. The video footage of the shooting showed that several people around the shooter and the victim could have witnessed the shooter holding his gun and raising it a few times before actually taking aim. None of them did, however, because they were all engrossed in their mobile devices.

Singin' the Social Media Blues

I mentioned in Chapter Two: Friending Is Trending that most peo-ple don't want to see a lot of negative reports on social media. We have become accustomed to seeing mostly rosy statements and pho-tos posted on social networks. I do think that is beginning to change slightly, but I don't envision social media to become a place where everyone sits around and complains either. As I explained before, most people don't want to see repeated complaining. Positivity is sup-posed to breed more positivity, so we post what we think others want to see. The flip side of this is that some people then become depressed when comparing their lives to the overly upbeat stories they are seeing online, even though they should realize they are only seeing partial pictures of other peoples' lives.

Some universities have begun to study the relationship between social media and mood. I don't doubt there is a relationship, but I'm not sure we have seen any truly conclusive studies at this point to determine whether the media itself actually has any more of an effect than if you received a bunch of postcards from friends taking fabulous trips on spring break. My assumption is that it's the volume of information we're receiving—not the information itself—that causes the problems. If I see one person post that she just went on a fabulous vacation, I'm happy for her. If I see twenty, I'm going to start wishing I were on vacation. I think it's an economies of scale problem.

That said, depression is a real disease and must be taken seriously. I've suffered from depression, so I know what it can do. Mine was mostly triggered by seasonal affective disorder, brought on by gray skies and lack of sunshine and Vitamin D. Once I figured this out, it became easier to combat my depression with natural light, a special-prescription bright light, vitamins, and upbeat music. I look at social media blues in the way I look at gray skies. If it causes you to be depressed, turn it off. If seeing everyone else's happy posts is too much for you, go read a book. We all need to recharge.

Ergonomic Injuries— Too Much Physical Time Online

Most of the computers, devices, and software we use were not designed with women or children in mind as the primary users. Most have been designed by men and for men, and they are generally not tested extensively for effects over time. The long-term effects of these devices—particularly mobile devices like smartphones and tablets—are not yet known.

I was injured from computing device overuse as a young adult. My first job after college was as a contract network engineer working on administering and securing business and government networks. I worked at a variety of different workstations each week, using complicated keyboard combinations to edit computer files. Before the end of my first year on the job, I had developed severe repetitive strain injuries that still plague me today. I had to quit my job at the time, and I spent a lot of time and money on physical therapy, changing my entire way of working. I lost several years of potential income as I recovered. I gradually began consulting and writing again, but I still suffer from some pain when using computers today, particularly if I type for long periods without breaks. Repetitive strain injuries are unfortunately all too common.

After repeated computer and mobile use, you can easily end up with eyestrain, tendinitis, tennis elbow, strained muscles, carpal tunnel syndrome, and other injuries. It's easy to say, "It won't happen to me." But it did happen to me, and I can look back and see all of the factors that contributed:

- I used the computer for extended periods of time.
- I rarely took breaks.
- I didn't have a correct ergonomic setup.
- The systems I was using and my chair and desk were not designed for people with my small frame.
- I worked in a cold work environment.
- I contorted my hands regularly to use the muscles in unnatural ways to do complicated key combinations (not unlike some that are required in some computer games).
- I kept working through the pain once it started, and it only got worse.

When I began using mobile phones extensively, I knew it was probably only a matter of time before my wrists started causing me pain again. I could tell by the way the iPhone was designed that it would bother me long term, and I was right. In early 2013, I began having finger pain. I eventually traced it to three things: the way I was holding my iPhone, the tapping I did in some apps on the iPhone, and the combined use of the trackpad on my laptop. I dramatically reduced my use of my iPhone and got an external mouse, so that helped a lot, but this should not be something that has to be tackled always on the user end.

Here are some ergonomic practices that you and your family can adopt that might help reduce the likelihood of repetitive strain injuries:

- If something hurts, stop doing it.
- Switch hands.
- Modify devices.
- Alternate activities.
- Take breaks.
- Limit overall time with devices.

I foresee more future injuries from mobile device use—especially in teens and young adults. Please be careful.

Are You Addicted to Social Media?

I've had e-mail capabilities since 1989. Before then, I used BBSes to exchange messages, so I've been communicating through some sort of online messaging system since 1987. I don't remember much about how I communicated before then, but I definitely developed early messaging habits at age fourteen. Learning a new technology can happen slowly, like it does for most people when they start using Twitter, or it can happen quickly, where you join a site like Facebook and suddenly you just have to check it every day to see what your friends are saying.

Either way, these habits develop over time. Some habits are healthy; others are unhealthy. Randi Zuckerberg, author of *Dot Complicated*, explains: "When somebody 'likes' something you do, your brain receives a little burst of dopamine, a chemical that the brain produces to indicate a reward. That's what makes our gadgets so addictive. Every time we get a notification, we're hoping for another hit."

We can joke about how easy it is to get sucked into digital media, surfing, trolling, refreshing for hours on end, but all this time online can lead to problems. Sometimes the habits arise from a fear of missing out (FOMO). Other times, it can go to extremes. I came across this tweet one day recently from Ted Weinstein, a Bay Area literary agent: "Best cellphone foul yet: almost walked into by a guy texting while walking on trail in coastal redwood forest!" If you get to the point where you can't even disconnect long enough to stop and smell the redwoods (or see the forest through the trees . . . choose the metaphor that works for you), it's time to stop, turn off the phone, and reboot yourself.

According to Kathleen Baird-Murray in *British Vogue*, "MRI brain scans of Internet addicts in China have revealed a disruption to connections in nerve fibers linking brain areas involved in emotions, decision-making, and self-control. . . . In America, they're considering adding 'Internet-use disorder' to the *Diagnostic and Statistical Manual of Mental Disorders*." If you think you need help, more therapists are becoming attuned to these problems as they become a prevalent issue in our society. A Pennsylvania hospital recently opened the first treatment program specifically for Internet addiction.

Digital Detox—Time to Unplug

The headline said it all: "Tourist falls off Australia pier while checking Facebook." In December of last year, a woman walking down a pier in Melbourne was so distracted that she literally walked off the pier, plunged into the water, and needed to be rescued. She didn't even know how to swim. We've all seen people nearly bump into each other on the street, but this took the problem to a new level. When the police pulled her out of the water, she was still clutching her phone. We can all use this as a lesson to unplug—especially on vacation!

Toward the end of 2012, my husband and I decided to take a two-week trip back to London over the Christmas and New Year holidays. Knowing it would be a long time away from home, work, and all of our pressing responsibilities, I opted to go on an e-mail hiatus. Other than our honeymoon, I can't recall going off e-mail for that long in the past decade. I still brought my laptop on the trip so we could search online for local information and activities, and I used my iPhone to post trip photos to Facebook and Instagram, occasionally checking Twitter for news, but I cut my online time down to about 10 percent of what it was on an average day at home.

The first couple of days felt weird. I kept reaching for my phone, wanting to check e-mail out of habit, but then I realized I didn't need or want to do so, and I turned off the phone. After that, I got into a rhythm, as did my husband, who turned off work e-mail and only responded to urgent family messages. We settled into a new routine on the trip, and, when we got home, it was somewhat painful to reenter the world of 500 e-mail messages a day. I didn't miss that at all.

Clay Johnson, author of *The Information Diet*, compares modern information consumption to junk food consumption. "Conscious consumption of information is possible," he argues, but it takes effort. We all use the Internet and digital media tools in different ways, and we each respond uniquely to change. So if you get to the point where you are overwhelmed by your online activities, make sure you alter your habits in a way that works with your lifestyle, not against it. Regardless of how you proceed, acknowledging that you have become overloaded is the first step.

Maximizing Your Digital Day

I don't measure my time online—at least not most of it. I measure time I spend on particular business activities, but, in general, I look at the Web as an outgrowth of my offline life, so I'm not going to be too hypercritical. That said, I only have a little time in my day that I can devote to personal pursuits online, so I'm not worried about too much screen time or overuse of various tools. Other than the rare Pinterest injury from staying up too late pinning pretty home-decorating photos, I'm pretty safe. But I've been online more than thirty years now, and I know my limits.

Here are a few quick tips for maximizing your time online: First, if you want others to see what you're posting, post when others are online. Seems obvious, but sometimes people don't think about that. Most social networks are active during the workday, but some

Overcoming Social Media Overuse

In order to save time, I'm combining all of the problems related to overuse, overstimulation, overload, dependence, depression, anxiety, addiction into one term for our purposes: SMOD, for Social Media Overuse Disorder. Clay Shirky, author of *Here Comes Everybody*, writes, "It's not information overload. It's filter failure." Keeping that in mind, how will you change the filters you put on your time, your habits, and your use of online tools, websites, and mobile apps?

Here are some ways to tackle SMOD:

- **Selective avoidance:** Decide that you cannot manage all of the information coming at you, so you will have to avoid some of it. Select some parts to deal with or respond to directly, and let the rest slide by (I do this with Twitter, for example—I can't possibly read tweets from the 4000-plus people I follow, so I don't try; instead, I consciously check the stream whenever I can).

- **Quit cold turkey:** Completely stop using applications that take too much of your time without providing enough benefit (games, for example, are easy to stop playing cold turkey, although more people are deciding they want off social networks now).

- **File it away:** Put whatever information is overwhelming you somewhere to deal with it later, aka temporary avoidance (this works with non-urgent e-mail messages, Facebook requests, LinkedIn invitations, and such).

- **Take a break:** This can mean a short break, like the phone-stack game, where everyone stacks their phones on the table for dinner, taking a whole day off once a week and engaging in a weekly "Technology Shabbat," as Tiffany Shlain calls it, or taking a weekend digital detox retreat. Share that you're unplugging via #unplug so you have accountability.

- **Forced moderation:** Apps that take control of your computer or device, limiting the amount you can use them . . . under your control, of course; you can always disable the apps (this is good for work environments where you don't want to get sidetracked spending too much time on social networks).

- **Timer method:** This one works for kids, so why not for adults? Give yourself a finite amount of time to do a task online, and stick to it (works well for dealing with important e-mail and daily checking of social networks).

- **Find an antidote:** For me, the antidote is nature—getting outside and taking a walk, generally alone. This allows me to recharge. I'm an introvert, so that works for me. If you're an extrovert, maybe your antidote would be going out with friends and leaving your cell phone in your handbag.

- **Rein it in:** This is where filters come in. You can start controlling your information by changing the way it comes at you, by reducing the number of mobile alerts you receive, turning off notifications within apps, filtering e-mail, and changing e-mail list subscriptions to batch mode (several delivered at once vs. each sent individually) so you deliberately curate your information flow.

- **Choosing the winners:** Taking a strategic approach, you can actually analyze your return on investment (ROI) of your time, looking at what you spend your time doing online and seeing how much of that time turns into positive experiences, professional opportunities, etc., and you can choose only to participate online in the places where you have the greatest return.

- **Attack:** For those brave souls who want to face their problems head-on, "Climb Every Mountain" style, you can just decide to take action and dive into your data deluge, only taking deep breaths until you get it under control (I do this periodically with e-mail, but it requires reserving a big chunk of time).

- **Dump it:** Trash. Delete. Do what you must. Get rid of it. Life is short.

peak during evenings. It's easy enough to find out this information if you do a quick search online. I also have some great infographics on my Pinterest "Social Media" pin board (pinterest.com/segranger/social-media/) that identify current most active times of the day online. There will always be random traffic spikes if there's a major event or big international news online, but generally traffic patterns are predictable.

For example, if you really want to be productive working on something online and not get interrupted by e-mail, work on the weekend. I saw a recent tweet from a blogger friend, Aimee Giese (@Greeblemonkey): "Saturday morning Twitter is so nice. 75 percent less links." Again, it goes back to your goals. What do you want to do online? It's not just about where; it's also about when, and for how long. Everything in this book has been recommended for a reason. If that reason doesn't match or fit with your life, perhaps you don't need to take the time to try it.

Are You Getting Post-Happy?
Volume and Timing

I often get asked questions about how often to post on social networks. There's no one-size-fits-all answer because the people on each social network will have different preferences. I think, at minimum, you should post to social media once a week if you want to stay active and informed online, but this is a personal choice. I worry more about oversaturating my friends and followers, so as a general rule, I say less is more. Don't post anywhere more than ten times a day, and spread it out throughout the day. I personally try to limit Facebook posts to once or twice a day, for example, because I know my friends don't want to see any more than that. On Twitter, if I go beyond five per day, I start losing followers. On Pinterest, people unfollow me if I blast them with more than fifteen images in succession. I've learned these things through trial and error; it could change in six months.

First, ask yourself: How often do I want to post? Then ask: How often does my community really want to hear from me? The best advice I can give is: Experiment with different times of day, volume of posting, and social networks in general. See what works for you. See what you like and dislike. See what causes people to unfollow you. See what types of content your friends and colleagues like to see most. If it's important to you how others respond, since the essence of social media is connecting with others, then you might want to alter how often you post. If it's more important to you that you post photos you like so you can come back and view them later, for example, then who cares if you post fifty in one day as long as it makes you happy? Try not to get hung up on numbers or frequency.

The Art and Science of Social Media Curation

Online etiquette matters. There are some unofficial rules when it comes to sharing on social media, and I've tried to make many of them as plain as possible. Some behaviors you learn by doing; others you learn by example. We've covered a lot of what to post, why to post, and when to post, but I haven't explained much yet about how often. I consider this a combination of art and science. I'll explain the art, then the science.

Following the rule that "content is king," let's assume that, if you're writing brilliant content, everyone will want to read it. This is true—to a point. If you're blasting everyone with fascinating information all day, even though it's amazing, eventually it will become overwhelming. That's why the term "curation" has become so prevalent when it comes to online content. Now, because of all of the information we have flowing toward and around us at all parts of our day online, we need that information curated, personalized, targeted, catered, or whatever term(s) you choose to use to make it right for you and your audience.

Here's where trends come in handy. Looking at general web trends, we find that the average blog post can be viewed indefinitely online. Facebook posts generally last around three hours for the average Facebook feed, but with Facebook's complex algorithms, more popular posts can linger longer. For Twitter, depending on how many people your average follower follows, the life of a tweet may only be a half hour or an hour, even though it's logged forever online. You also have to consider what kind of reach or traction you receive by posting on these social networks, and you have to think about how much time you put into them. I generally only spend several seconds composing most tweets, but, on rare occasion, I've spent a half hour agonizing over them. It all depends on how important the content is to you.

I also suggest compartmentalizing social media use. I personally don't often post the same content on different social networks. I try to use them independently in a way that takes the most advantage of their assets. That allows me to maintain a greater appreciation for their unique features. Twitter keeps me informed 24/7. Facebook keeps me in touch with many more friends than I could have ever kept up with on my own. Instagram reminds me to appreciate small things. Pinterest helps me find visual representations of whatever I'm seeking. Linkedin helps me track my professional connections. Slideshare teaches me interesting new ideas. Google Plus allows me to keep tabs on new technologies. YouTube provides hours of video entertainment. While I will share the same information on different networks, I try to do it at different times, and in ways that allow for that media to best be appreciated in that forum.

Final Thoughts:
Determining Your Digital Future

I first envisioned writing this book in 2011, when it became apparent to me that many people were struggling with the challenges of adjusting to their increasingly digital lives. During the past three years as I've been researching, writing, and revising this book, I've watched Facebook, LinkedIn, and Twitter all become public companies and household names. I've seen new social networks designed around sharing photos and videos, allowing anyone to become a photojournalist or filmmaker. And I've watched countless times as people from all over the world have come together to help each other online in times of need. We are all becoming content creators and curators, community managers, and agents of change. At the same time, the cultures of our digital world and our physical world are rapidly fusing together.

News coverage now regularly includes stories of people and their daily lives online. Comedians regularly make jokes about social media. Seventy-year-olds use "google" as a verb. Lovers text sweet nothings through emoticons. Teenagers use hashtags in air quotes as humor. Trolling Facebook has become a regular part of our day. Today's Internet, no longer suspect or mysterious, has become a trusted partner. The digital mystique no longer comes from the elusive unknown; now its intrigue exists as much from the people and communities online as the technologies that brought us there. You and I are empowered to achieve our dreams because we've chosen to be part of this unprecedented transformation.

As you continue developing your own digital life, I hope you will remember some of the important messages from this book: You can define your image online and decide what you show about yourself. You can reach out to the ones you love, and find new ways to share with them. You can empower the next generation and teach them how to experience the fullness of the Internet in the best way possible. You can determine the digital legacy you want to leave. You can build, nurture, and support the communities that are meaningful to you. And you can make a difference in the lives of others, harnessing the power of those communities.

Now this culture of connectedness has woven itself into the fabric of your life, as it has altered the tapestry of our world, irreversibly changing how we all live. I hope you will seize this opportunity to empower yourself and enhance your life. You never know where it could lead.

Algorithm – an equation or set of rules and steps used to solve a particular type of problem or to serve a need, such as inside a software application

Analytics – applications or tools that measure various data metrics for websites or social networks, often including statistical analyses

Avatar – cartoon-like image representing a user, displayed in place of a profile photo

BBS – Bulletin Board System, the precursor to today's websites, blogs and social sites

Big Data – Collections of data so enormous that managing and processing the data requires specialized solutions

Bitcoin – a type of unit of digital monetary currency

Blog – (shortened from web log) an online publication generally written in journal-like form, with a casual tone; the difference between blogs and other written digital media is that comments are typically allowed

Bot – an automated software program, like a virtual robot, that repeatedly collects information from and/or sends information to websites, which can include auto-posting comments on blogs or other social networks

Cloud – virtual storage, essentially for data located on offsite servers

CRM – Customer Relationship Management; a model for tracking customer relationships and contacts

Creative Commons – an organization and process by which content creators can license their works in flexible terms, allowing for full sharing capabilities or with attribution vs. traditional copyright

Crowd Fund – process for funding projects by asking / inviting others to participate as funders, generally through a service like Kickstarter or Indiegogo

Crowdsource – process for asking for advice from a wide range of people online

Curate – to selectively compile a collection of content for a distinct theme or purpose

Cybercitizen – person who resides in or is active online

Cyberspace – the ethereal world of the Internet, online, anywhere that's a part of the digital world

Cyberstalker – an online stalker

Domain Name – a unique name for a website so we don't all have to remember virtual locations with numbers like 74.125.239.101

Emoticon – a smiley or other symbol approx. the size of text characters, used to show emotion accompanying text comments

Feed – a data format for web content, so that it can easily be shared or fed to others, i.e. a blog feed, news feed or a Twitter feed

FOMO – Fear of Missing Out

Geolocating – the act of locating a device through its physical location, using trackable technology embedded inside the device

Godwin's Law – an Internet adage coined by Mike Godwin – "as an online discussion grows longer, the probability of a comparison involving Nazis or Hitler approaches 1"

Google – not just a company, Google has become a verb – to google someone is to look them up online, regardless of whether you're actually using Google's search tools

Hactivism – using computer hacking tools and techniques for activism

Handle – alias or nickname used on a social media account

Hashtag – a term used for searching and tracking terms on a variety of social networks, with a pound # sign in front of it, i.e. #TDMBook

Internet of Things – the concept that more things are connected to the Internet than people, such as computers, smart phones, e-readers, and health monitors, comprising another level of connectivity

IRL – acronym for In Real Life

Meme – an idea or theme that spreads through cultural use; for our purposes, via digital media

MOOC – Massive Open Online Course, a course available online for large numbers of students, often free, open to anyone, sometimes reaching thousands of students

Open Data – sets of collected or compiled information that have been provided to the general public for various uses

Open Source – a model for software development that allows for anyone to participate in the process, following the theory that more ideas are better than one, the best ideas rise to the top, and that software is most secure when it can be tested by many developers

Page – a web page, primary content shown on a website, generally static content (vs. a blog *post* that tends to be dynamic)

Paywall – virtual wall behind which premium or other digital content is held until payment is first received to read or view that content

Phishing – tricky attempts to gather personal information from users, such as a fake e-mail message saying one's bank password needs to be changed, prompting the user to unwittingly supply confidential information to criminals; phishing is rampant

Post – a post is a chunk of digital content, usually on an actively changing platform like a blog or a social network; to post is a verb for the act of publishing online

Rule 34 – a meme saying that for any thing or idea, somewhere online there will be porn involving it

Selfie – photo of oneself, generally taken with a smart phone, posted online

SEO – Search Engine Optimization – the act of configuring websites or other online content to be as searchable as possible, so people can find it easily

Slactivism – so-called lazy person's activism or action easily achieved online to make oneself feel better, like changing one's avatar to an image representing a particular cause

Spam – e-mail, comments or other digital messages generally sent by unwanted sources, like companies or campaigns, without permission and/or to excess

Stream – similar to a feed, a stream can be of any form of data, but is more generally used in reference to audio or video

TLA – three letter acronym; common in the world of texting, i.e. LOL and TMI

TMI – too much information

Troll – digital entity (sometimes a person, sometimes a bot) that posts comments online in a typically purposeful attempt at provoking an emotional response, generally negative

Tweet – a short post on Twitter that must be completed in 140 characters or less

Unfriend – the act of removing someone as a 'friend' on Facebook or other social network

Vaguebook – posting intentionally vague information on Facebook

Vanity Search – an online search to discover what information is posted about you online; although called a vanity search, it's actually a savvy tactic to ensure that anything published online about you is accurate

RECOMMENDED READING

Boyd, Danah. *It's Complicated: The Social Lives of Networked Teens.* Yale University Press, 2014.

Carr, Nicholas. *The Shallows: What the Internet Is Doing to Our Brains.* W. W. Norton & Company, 2011.

Carvin, Andy. *Distant Witness: Social Media, the Arab Spring, and a Journalism Revolution.* CUNY Journalism Press, 2013.

Cohen, Jared, and Eric Schmidt. *The New Digital Age: Reshaping the Future of People, Nations and Business.* Knopf, 2013.

Davis, Laurie. *Love at First Click: The Ultimate Guide to Online Dating.* Atria Books, 2013.

Fine, Allison. *Momentum: Igniting Social Change in the Connected Age.* Jossey-Bass, 2006.

Fine, Allison, and Beth Kanter. *The Networked Nonprofit: Connecting with Social Media to Drive Change.* Jossey-Bass, 2010.

Ghonim, Wael. *Revolution 2.0: The Power of the People Is Greater Than the People in Power: A Memoir.* Houghton Mifflin Harcourt, 2012.

Ivester, Matt. *lol...OMG!: What Every Student Needs to Know About Online Reputation Management, Digital Citizenship and Cyberbullying*. CreateSpace Independent Publishing Platform, 2011.

Izquierdo, Calandra, and Lazarus Potter. *Textiquette: the Do's and Do Nots of Texting*. CreateSpace Independent Publishing Platform, 2013.

Johnson, Clay A. *The Information Diet: A Case for Conscious Consumption*. O'Reilly Media, 2012.

Kapin, Allyson, and Amy Sample Ward. *Social Change Anytime Everywhere: How to Implement Online Multichannel Strategies to Spark Advocacy, Raise Money, and Engage Your Community*. Jossey-Bass, 2013.

Kanter, Beth, and Katie Delahaye Paine. *Measuring the Networked Nonprofit: Using Data to Change the World*. Jossey-Bass, 2012.

Keen, Andrew. *Digital Vertigo: How Today's Online Social Revolution Is Dividing, Diminishing, and Disorienting Us*. St. Martin's Griffin, 2013.

Lindsay, John. *Emails from an A**hole: Real People Being Stupid*. Sterling, 2010.

Lupold Bair, Amy. *Raising Digital Families For Dummies*. For Dummies, 2013.

Mele, Nicco. *The End of Big: How the Internet Makes David the New Goliath*. St. Martin's Press, 2013.

Merchant, Nilofer. *11 Rules for Creating Value in the Social Era*. Harvard Business Review Press, 2012.

Newsom, Gavin, and Lisa Dickey. *Citizenville: How to Take the Town Square Digital and Reinvent Government.* The Penguin Press HC, 2013.

Rheingold, Howard. *Net Smart: How to Thrive Online.* The MIT Press, 2012.

Rushkoff, Douglas. *Present Shock: When Everything Happens Now.* Penguin Group, 2013.

——— *Program or Be Programmed: Ten Commands for a Digital Age.* Soft Skull Press, 2011.

Shipley, David, and Will Schwalbe. *SEND: Why People Email So Badly and How to Do It Better.* Vintage, 2010.

Shirky, Clay. *Here Comes Everybody: The Power of Organizing Without Organizations.* Penguin Press, 2008.

Steyer, James P. *Talking Back to Facebook: The Common Sense Guide to Raising Kids in the Digital Age.* Scribner, 2012.

Turkle, Sherri. *Alone Together: Why We Expect More from Technology and Less from Each Other.* Basic Books, 2012.

Webb, Amy. *Data, A Love Story: How I Gamed Online Dating to Meet My Match.* Dutton Adult Publishers, 2013.

Winters, Charles, and Anne Winters. *The Official Book of Electronic Etiquette.* Skyhorse Publishing, 2010.

Zandt, Deanna. *Share This!: How You Will Change the World with Social Networking.* Berrett-Koehler Publishers, 2010.

Zittrain, Jonathan. *The Future of the Internet—And How to Stop It.* Yale University Press, 2009.

Zuckerberg, Randi. *Dot Complicated: Untangling Our Wired Lives.* HarperOne, 2013.

Zuckerman, Ethan. *Rewire: Digital Cosmopolitans in the Age of Connection.* W. W. Norton & Company, 2013.

ACKNOWLEDGMENTS

This book could not have happened without the enduring support of my family: my daughter, Julia Pletcher, who inspires me daily, my husband, Chuck Pletcher, who has encouraged my writing for twenty years, my mother, Verna Granger, who always has a kind word and a keen proofreading eye, my sister, Carmel Granger, who researched, edited, and helped me stay sane, her husband, Greg Stoehr, for going above and beyond the call of duty as a courier for various versions of the book, and my cousin, Laura Davis, whose editorial insight and sense of humor helped me through a few rough writing patches.

To Laura Mazer, the executive editor at Seal Press, thank you for taking a chance on me and this book. To developmental editor Rachel Sarah, copyeditor Barrett Briske, publicist Jesse Wentworth, designer Domini Dragoone, and everyone at Seal Press and the Perseus Books Group that helped make this possible, thank you so much. You all taught me a great deal. To my literary agent, Linda Konner, a big thanks for taking a chance on an unusual project, and to my publicist, Sylvia Paull, continued appreciation for keeping a close eye on technology networks, trends, and always giving me the full scoop without any sugar coating. Huge thanks to Danielle Stenblom, my research assistant, for burning the midnight oil and keeping Julia entertained. Thanks to Mark Bennington, photographer, for my headshot. And of course I have to thank my friend Elisa Camahort Page for taking time out of her busy schedule running BlogHer to write the foreword.

Thank you so much to friends and others who shared stories, inspiration, research:

Anne-Marie Fowler, IdaRose Sylvester, Beth Blecherman, Jaelithe Judy, Shaun Dakin, Samantha Matalone Cook, Kaari Jacobs, Mark Ardayfio, Cynthia Samuels, Jen Lee Reeves, Ian Thomson, Lois Kauffman, Anastasia Ashman, Maria Ross, Erin Kotecki Vest, Michelle Kraus, Shasta Nelson, Brooke Moreland, Laz Potter, Beki Hastings, Morra Aarons-Mele, Gretchen Curtis, Beth Kanter, Kalen Gallagher, Enoch Choi, Pamela Hornik, Cynthia Liu, Glennia Campbell, Melinda Byerley, Katya Obukhova, Adam Nash, Beth Leeman-Markowski, Cyrus Krohn, Ben Huh, Julie Peters, Tracy Russo, and Cindy Sorley. Thanks also to those who provided anonymous anecdotes.

To other champions of my writing and work who helped me build the self confidence to embark on this journey—Tatyana Kanzaveli, Catherine Marcus, Amanda Enayati, Rebecca Rodskog, Katie Jacobs Stanton, Lucie Newcomb, Alix Mayer—your collective energy kept me going when I felt like I'd never get there. To other author and editor friends who advised me—Simon St. Laurent, Michelle Lamar, Cory Doctorow, Denise Brosseau, Deanna Zandt, Lisa Stahr, Joanne Bamberger, Kapil Raina, Tekla Perry, Nilofer Merchant, and everyone in the Authoress group—I hope I can return the favor sometime. And to all of my blogger friends and Facebook friends who encouraged me and helped me crowdsource my ideas for the book, thank you for your kindness and enthusiasm.

Big thanks to Larry Page and Sergey Brin for the best research tool in the world, and thanks to Apple computer for making awesome laptops and mobile devices that allowed me to write and research this book. Thanks also to the staff members at Coupa Café, Starbucks Ranco, and Bumble Los Altos for providing tea, wifi, and workspace.

Finally, since this is my first book, I have to thank my ninth-grade English teacher, Ms. Bramley, who took me aside and advised me to keep writing and to stay true to my authentic voice. Thank you all!

ABOUT THE AUTHOR

Sarah Granger first ventured into the digital world in 1982 as a curious nine-year-old. By age fourteen, she had established an online community in her hometown of Kansas City. Since then, she has become a renowned digital media innovator and journalist focused on the impact of information technology on our lives. In 2012, she was recognized as one of the "40 Under 40" rising stars by *The Silicon Valley Business Journal*.

Sarah has spent the past decade advising business and nonprofit leaders and their organizations on how to improve digital outreach to their customers and communities. She has also engaged in technology policy issues such as electronic privacy, cybersecurity, gender equality online, and civic data sharing. She founded the Center for Technology, Media and Society to pursue projects in these areas.

Sarah's writing has appeared in numerous publications, including *Forbes, Harvard Business Review, SFGate, BlogHer,* and *The Huffington Post*. She has written hundreds of articles and blogs, several scripts, and a handful of book chapters. She has also helped launch more than two dozen digital publications for organizations and collaborative groups.

A graduate of the University of Michigan, Sarah's lectures, keynotes, and workshops have been delivered to colleges and conferences around the world. Sarah has been featured on *CBS News*, *Good Morning America*, and *National Public Radio*. She lives in Los Altos, California, with her husband, daughter, and three rambunctious rescue cats.

Stay in touch with Sarah at www.sarahgranger.com.

Selected Titles from Seal Press

Reality Bites Back: The Troubling Truth About Guilty Pleasure TV, by Jennifer L. Pozner. $16.95, 978-1-58005-265-8. Deconstructs reality TV's twisted fairytales to demonstrate that they are far from being simple "guilty pleasures," and arms readers with the tools they need to understand and challenge the stereotypes reality TV reinforces.

She's Such a Geek: Women Write About Science, Technology, and Other Nerdy Stuff, edited by Annalee Newitz and Charlie Anders. $14.95, 978-1-58005-190-3. From comic books and gaming to science fiction and blogging, nerdy women have their say in this witty collection that takes on the "boys only" clubs and celebrates a woman's geek spirit.

What Will It Take to Make a Woman President?: Conversations About Women, Leadership, and Power, by Marianne Schnall. $16.00, 978-1-58005-496-6. This timely discussion features interviews with more than twenty leading politicians, writers, artists, and activists about why America has not yet elected a female president.

Airbrushed Nation: The Lure and Loathing of Women's Magazines, by Jennifer Nelson. $17.00, 978-1-58005-413-3. Jennifer Nelson—a longtime industry insider—exposes the naked truth behind the glossy pages of women's magazines, both good and bad.

How to Woo a Jew: The Modern Jewish Guide to Dating and Mating, by Tamar Caspi. $17.00, 978-1-58005-500-0. Advice for Jewish men and women on finding a soul mate from JDate's dating expert.

Got Teens?: The Doctor Moms' Guide to Sexuality, Social Media and Other Adolescent Realities, by Logan Levkoff, PhD, and Jennifer Wider, MD. $16.00, 978-1-58005-506-2. Adolescent health and sexuality experts provide parents of middle schoolers a way to decode their teen's health questions and behavior.

Find Seal Press Online
www.SealPress.com
www.Facebook.com/SealPress
Twitter: @SealPress